Columbia University

Contributions to Education

Teachers College Series

No. 104

AMS PRESS
NEW YORK

THE EDUCATION OF GIRLS IN CHINA

BY

IDA BELLE LEWIS, Ph.D.

TEACHERS COLLEGE, COLUMBIA UNIVERSITY
CONTRIBUTION TO EDUCATION, NO. 104

PUBLISHED BY
Teachers College, Columbia University
NEW YORK CITY
1919

Library of Congress Cataloging in Publication Data

Lewis, Ida Belle, 1887-
   The education of girls in China.

   Reprint of the 1919 ed., issued in series: Teachers
College, Columbia University. Contributions to edu-
cation, no. 104.
   Originally presented as the author's thesis, Columbia.
   Bibliography: p.
   1. Education of women--China. I. Title.
II. Series: Columbia University. Teachers College.
Contributions to education, no. 104.
LC2312.L4 1972   376'.951   78-176992
ISBN 0-404-55104-1

Reprinted by Special Arrangement with Teachers
College Press, New York, New York

From the edition of 1919 , New York
First AMS edition published in 1972
Manufactured in the United States

AMS PRESS, INC.
NEW YORK, N. Y.   10003

TO MY
FATHER AND MOTHER

PREFACE

This study of The Education of Girls in China has been made possible only by the coöperation of many friends, Chinese and American, in this country and in China. All have given unsparingly of their time and advice, and to each one the writer acknowledges her indebtedness.

Especially is gratitude due to Mr. T. H. Fu, the Minister of Education of China, and to Mr. T. T. Wang and Mr. U. Y. Yen of the Educational Mission at Washington for courteous supply of rare documents and generous answers to all requests for information; to Mr. E. W. Wallace, Miss Mary Louise Hamilton, Miss Jennie Baird Bridenbaugh, Miss Lydia Trimble and Miss Elizabeth Farries for gathering questionnaires from several centers in China; to Dr. I. T. Headland and Professor S. C. Kiang for permitting the use of unpublished manuscript; to Mr. W. T. Tao and Mr. T. H. Cheng for much translation and many suggestions in gathering material; to Bishop W. S. Lewis, of China, Dr. I. L. Kandel, and the Misses Clara and Laura Chassell for criticism and reading of manuscript. To Professor G. D. Strayer, Professor Paul Monroe, Dr. T. H. P. Sailer and Professor Willystone Goodsell, of Teachers College, the writer is indebted for guidance and inspiration throughout the work.

I. B. L.

CONTENTS

THE EDUCATION OF GIRLS IN CHINA

INTRODUCTION

Education in China has for many centuries been a basic factor in nation and society. Before 1901–03,[1] under the examination system, education in the classics was the route by which the poorest lad in the most remote village might become the highest official in the realm. To win a degree, and thus bring honor to parents and village, was the epitome of filial piety and social service. The lettered man, by sheer virtue of his knowledge, has always received from the entire population a deep, almost reverent respect. Education consisted mainly of a mastery of the classics.[2] Since the discovery of printing,[3] each succeeding generation in China has added to its literature of written tradition, history, poetry and philosophy. The people thus crystallized the ideals which they wrought out through experience. This literature, especially the Five Classics and the Four Books, has had a tremendous influence in the life of the country. Memorized and expounded, the classics were the only text-books of the schools. Scholars deepened their thought by meditation upon the words of the sages. Morality was measured by that of the ancients. From the city on the coast to the tiny village near the headwaters of the Yangtze, political, family and individual life was consciously tested by the principles of the Sacred Books of the Middle Kingdom. Ethical relationship and right conduct is the theme of the classics, and was the chief subject of thought and discussion before the modern era in education.

The new education, which introduced science, modern history, and, in mission schools, the Bible, from the West over seventy-five years ago,[4] has been a powerful force in recent social and political change. Throughout the entire nation its effects are evident in bringing about progressive movements.

---

[1] Kuo, P. W., *The Chinese System of Public Education*, p. 78.

[2] *Ibid.*, pp. 34–35.

[3] Fu Hsi (2852 B. C.) the traditional inventor of Chinese writing and founder of Chinese history. See Pott, F. L., *Sketch of Chinese History*, p. 10.

[4] *Ibid.*, p. 4.

As a result of these conflicting ideals of education, in every Chinese community there are three definite social groups: the conservative, still dominated by the ancient educational traditions; the progressive, dominated by the ideals of modern education; and the changing, those who are moving from the old to the new.

The conservative group includes both the illiterate men and women and the scholar of the ancient classics. The scholars wield great influence in their own communities. They often come into relationship with the District Magistrate, which makes them men of mark among their fellows. They are constantly called upon to assist in the settlement of disputes. At weddings and funerals, they are always in places of honor, due to their literary degrees.[1] Their ideals and social attitudes have been determined by the standards set forth in the ancient literature of China. Because they believe the golden age of China to have been in ancient times and that the present and the future of the nation depend upon copying closely the deeds of the ancients, although new social customs are being rapidly introduced about them, these men hold tenaciously to the past and conscientiously do their best to block change.

At the other extreme of the social scale, and yet exerting a tremendous influence on public opinion, are the illiterate artisans and farmers. These people cannot read. Quotations from the classics repeated to them by the village literati and bits of homely philosophy handed down by word of mouth from generation to generation are the bases for their intellectual and social life. Their travel is bounded by the neighboring villages. The welfare of China as a nation holds little meaning for them. They neither know nor care about politics beyond those of their own village.[2] Limited to this narrow horizon, each man is bound by a fierce economic pressure which forces him to work hard at his trade or on his farm from early dawn until dark. "Contrary to

---

[1] Smith, A. H., *Village Life in China*, pp. 132–133.

[2] Cf. Bashford, J. W., *China*, pp. 307–308. "The people have not been greatly interested in the national government . . . (because) . . . the general government did not confer any widespread and vital benefit upon the people." However, it may be that under the Republic the farmers might have known or heard of the election of representatives and the like. (Mr. T. H. Cheng.)

the theory of certain sociologists, this intensified struggle for life has no perceptible effect in promoting economic or social improvement. It makes for exertion and strain but not for progress, because the prime means of progress are inventions and discoveries, and it is just these that bondslaves to poverty, under the stress of the struggle to keep alive, are not able to bring forth."[1] "It will be at best a couple of lifetimes before the plane of existence of the common people will at all approximate that of the common people of America."[2] Starvation, debt, and beggary[3] are the alternatives to their deadening toil. Because of these circumstances the new ideas of progress can meet with little response from the great mass of the Chinese populace.

Another powerful conservative factor in society is illiterate womanhood. Confined to one village, unable to read, kept subservient until youth is over, superstitious, and fearful of everything new, the women of most households, in educated circles as well as among the middle and lower classes, are bound to the traditions of the locality. Mothers, to whom every child owes implicit obedience, refuse to allow their sons to attend progressive schools. If a child is sick, and the father calls a western trained physician who administers scientific medicine, the mother adds a dose of concoction guaranteed by the village medicine man in order to make rapid recovery more certain. Wives use their whole repertoire of schemes in order to thwart any project of their husbands which will involve experiment. These women are not to be blamed, for they are victims of a social system. But they hang like millstones upon the necks of their families. Until womankind be lifted up, China must needs be heavily weighted in her struggle for progress.

Opposed in thought and practice to the conservative element in Chinese society is an alert, progressive social group. The remarkable changes recently brought about in every phase of Chinese life have been the result of their work. Fearless, often radical, sometimes uncompromising, they have dared break the bonds of tradition, have questioned and denied the supremacy of

---

[1] Ross, E. A., *The Changing Chinese*, p. 92.

[2] *Ibid.*, p. 69.

[3] There are few beggars in a country region where there is no famine. Business failures, and the like, go to the city to beg.

the past over the present. They have even paid the price of unfilial conduct, when it has been necessary to bring about change. They have been educated in modern Chinese, Japanese, American, and European schools. They have travelled extensively and have brought home a changed conception of nation and society. In their open struggle towards democracy, they are pushing universal education, political freedom, economic progress and social reform. The men who belong to this group are the officials (often lesser officials because they are young men), the business men, the physicians, and the educators of China to-day. "A recent census of Chinese students in Peking who are returned students from Europe, America, and Japan shows that there are nearly 950 accounted for in that metropolis and that of these 806 are engaged in government service. They constitute 23.2 per cent of the total number of departmental officers, and in certain departments, such as the Department of Agriculture where special training is particularly valued, they number nearly half the total roll of employees. Of the returned students now in Peking, 522 are from Japan, 154 are from America, 99 are from Great Britain, 52 are from France, 47 are from Germany, 38 are from Belgium, 9 are from Austria-Hungary, 7 are from Russia, and 1 is from Spain. As to distribution in various departments, it is estimated that in the Ministry of War, 34.1 per cent of the total number of officials are returned students; in the Ministry of Education, 28.8 per cent; in the Forestry Bureau, 32.2 per cent; in the Ministry of Commerce, 48.6 per cent; in the National Supreme Court, 40 per cent; in the Ministry of Communications, 46.7 per cent. These men are leaders of New China."[1]

Women leaders have also a claim in the progress of China. During the Revolution equal suffrage was urged with much vigor and earnestness upon the new republic. Women are prominent in the Red Cross units of Shanghai and Tientsin, and doubtless of other cities. Many of the Chinese private schools are managed entirely by women. Contemporaneous literature is enriched by women's magazines, some of which are edited by women. Chinese women physicians stand out prominently in the medical world, and have made large contributions to the well being of

---

[1] *Chinese Students' Monthly*, Vol. XIII, No. 4, p. 193 (February, 1918).

North, Central, East and South China.[1] Women in institutions of learning in every province of China and in many colleges of America will carry on the movement which is bringing a new era for the women of their nation.

Between the conservative and progressive groups is a great proportion of the population. Touched by the new life and thought of the outside world, they are still deeply imbued with the spirit of Old China. They read the modern newspaper, but think it less important than the study of Chinese history. They allow their children to attend modern schools, but insist on home memorization of the classics; they permit sons to study in foreign lands, but arrange their betrothal with little or no regard for their wishes. Members of this group represent all stages of change between the old and the new; keen to recognize advantages and disadvantages in both the old and the new, they try to combine the best in both, to suit their own individual and family needs.

Advancement of the work, now done relatively unconsciously by the individuals of the changing group, is the task which confronts the modern educator of China. It is a task which must be accomplished consciously and with definite purposes. Both the old and the new civilizations contribute elements which are necessary to present educational effectiveness, but which are now to a great extent selected by tradition. The discovery and choice of content and methods of education which vary with the needs of the conservative, progressive and changing groups of society is an outstanding problem of education in China to-day. Within this problem, the education of boys and the education of girls are differentiated sharply in administration and to some extent in content. The purpose of this study is the survey of specific aspects of the problem that have to do with the nature of education offered to girls in China, the relation of the present educational program to the life of the nation, together with the general lines of change and experiment which will make this program more efficient.

---

[1] Dr. Hu King An, graduate of Philadelphia (1894), who has worked in South China; Dr. Yamei Kin, who for several years had charge of a government hospital in Tientsin; Dr. Mary Stone, Michigan (1896), who treated 19,649 patients in her hospital in Kiukiang in 1912; Dr. Ida Kahn, Michigan (1896), who has served with great success in her hospital in Nanchang, and later in the government hospital in Tientsin.

PART I

CHAPTER I

THE TRADITIONAL EDUCATION OF WOMEN

In the classics the great sages incorporated their ideals for the education of women, and each succeeding generation has accepted their doctrines in this, as in other fields. The Four Books for Girls, *Nu Chieh*, *Nei Hsun*, *Nu Lun Yu*, and the *Nu Fan Chieh Lu*, written by women, simplified and explained the doctrines of the classics concerning their sex, and have been used as text-books for the education of girls throughout succeeding generations. Thus the classics and these four books set for the women of China the standards of education which were unquestioned until the middle of the last century, and which even to-day dominate the thought and customs of women in the conservative classes.

The standards of moral education were filial piety and obedience to the husband, submission to the desires of brothers and sisters-in-law, and humility of spirit. Of these, the duty of filial piety was paramount. It was the root from which all Chinese society developed. Both sexes alike shared the obligation. Confucius made no distinction between men and women when he said, "Filial piety and fraternal submission, are they not the root of all benevolent actions?"[1] In her enumeration of woman's virtues, Jen Hsiao names filial piety as the first,[2] and claims that women as well as men may obtain it to a high degree. "Someone says, 'Such is the filial piety of holy men, women cannot attain to it.' This is not true. Filial piety and brotherly love are heaven given dispositions. How can there be a distinction between male and female?"[3] Ceremonials which ensure reverent service at rising and at meals, loving obedience in every detail of conduct, and filial anxiety for the constant welfare and happiness of parents are outlined in detail in the *Li*

---

[1] Confucius, *Analects*, Book I, Chap. II. Translated by J. Legge.
[2] Jen Hsiao, *Nei Hsun*, Chap. I. Translated by I. T. Headland.
[3] *Ibid.*, Chap. XII.

7

Ki,[1] one of the greatest of the classics. To incorporate such filial conduct into daily life was the most important duty of Chinese women.

The relation of husband and wife is based upon a fundamental philosophy of the Chinese people. "Great righteousness is shown in that man and woman occupy their correct places; the relative positions of Heaven and Earth,"[2] said the Book of Changes. Lady Tsao, speaking from the standpoint of a woman, agrees that "The Yin and the Yang, like the male and the female, are very different principles. The virtue of the Yang is firmness, the virtue of the Yin flexibility."[3] "If the husband is unworthy he cannot govern his wife. If the husband cannot govern his wife, the dignity of the household will be deficient. If the wife does not serve her husband, the rules of propriety will be destroyed."[4]

The relation of superior and inferior, however, does not intimate that the position of woman is to be despised, nor does it follow that marriage is lightly esteemed.[5] Mencius recognized marriage as "the greatest of human relationships."[6] Moreover, the wife was considered responsible for the conduct of her husband. Sung Jo Chao has thus set forth clearly her urgent duty, "If she finds him in error, she should earnestly reprove him."[7] Wang Chieh Fu stated that the success of certain emperors who became prosperous was due to the fact that they all had "virtuous and intelligent inside helpers."[8] The wife is not permitted, however, to marry again. "Once mated with her husband, all her life she will not change (her feeling of duty to him) and hence when the husband dies, she will not marry again."[9] "There is no second marriage ceremony for a wife."[10] Of course, this same

---

[1] *Li Ki*, Book X. Translated by J. Legge.

[2] Book of Changes, XXXVII, Kia Zan Heragram King Wan's Explanation. Treatise on Than. Translated by J. Legge.

[3] Lady Tsao, *Nu Chieh*, Chap. III. Translated by I. T. Headland.

[4] *Ibid.*, Chap. II.

[5] See *Li Ki*, Book IX, Sec. III:2.

[6] Mencius, Book V, Part I, Chap. II. Translated by J. Legge.

[7] Sung Jo Chao, *Nu Lun Yu*, Chap. VII. Translated by I. T. Headland.

[8] Wang Chieh Fu, *Nu Fan Chieh Lu*, Chap. I. Translated by I. T. Headland.

[9] *Li Ki*, Book IX, Sec. III:7.

[10] Lady Tsao, *Nu Chieh*, Chap. V.

standard did not apply to the husband. "If a wife dies the husband may marry again,"[1] says Lady Tsao, interpreting both the classics and general usage.[2] Nor was possession of concubines to be considered immoral. The classics recognize this system in many places.[3] The duty of each wife and concubine under this régime was to have love for each other, with no jealous feeling.

On the other hand, when the superiority of the husband, the duty of obedience on the part of the wife, and dignity of marriage were recognized by both husband and wife, happiness was set forth as the result, and, indeed, was often achieved. There are several love songs of rare sweetness and of high' idealism in the classic book of Odes.[4] A couplet from one of these poems pictures the beautiful home life:

> Loving union with wife and children
> Is like music with lutes.[5]

The fact that the wife was given the rank of the husband in the marriage ceremony brought her the duty of obedience to the elder brothers and their wives, but gave her the privilege of governing those who were younger.[6] Humanly speaking, this presented grave dangers for domestic peace; hence Lady Tsao advised: "Now to win the hearts of your younger brothers and sisters there is nothing better than humility and obedience. . . . If you understand these two things, you can agree exactly with them."[7]

The motive for the entire code of propriety was to be virtue, or humility of spirit. Mencius expressed the ideal by saying, "To look upon compliance as their correct course is the rule of women."[8] Lady Tsao writes: "She should be humble, yielding, modest and respectful. First others, then herself. When she

---

[1] Lady Tsao, *Nu Chieh*, Chap. V. Translated by I. T. Headland.

[2] Cf. Mencius, Book VII, Chap. VI.

[3] Book of Odes (*She King*), Part I, Book V:5. Translated by J. Legge. *Li Ki*, Book X, Sec. II:26, 37. Translated by J. Legge.

[4] Cf. Book of Odes (*She King*), Part II, Book VII, Ode IV. *Ibid.*, Part I, Book I, Ode I.

[5] *Ibid.*, Part II, Book I, Ode IV.

[6] *Li Ki*, Book X, Sec. I:18.

[7] Lady Tsao, *Nu Chieh*, Chap. VII.

[8] Mencius, Book III, Part II, Chap. II.

does good, she ought not to talk about it; when she does wrong, she ought not to excuse herself. Even if shame or disgrace are put upon her, she should be patient. She should be as careful at all times as if she were afraid."[1] And yet such conduct was found by experience to bring more than its own reward, for, says Lady Tsao, "I have never heard of a woman who possessed these . . . virtues who had occasion to grieve because she was unknown, or who fell into disfavor."[2] Jen Hsiao emphasized the fact that "virtue comes not from without. Its source is within."[3] "Even while alone you cannot afford to be careless of a single thought. You say, 'No one sees me.' Can you hide it from heaven? You say, 'No one knows it.' Do you deceive your own heart?"[4]

In spite of their inferior station in society, it was true in China, as in all ancient civilizations, that while women were illiterate they were not uneducated. The responsibilities of the home were heavy and called for many kinds of skill. Vocational standards were set high and the instruction which she received fitted the girl for such duties as were thought properly hers.

In common with all people, the Chinese believed the primary sphere of woman to be in her home. Here she was supreme. In fact, the *Li Ki* says, "The men should not speak of what belongs to the inside of the house," at the same time adding, "nor the woman of what belongs to the outside."[5]

Lady Tsao realized the weight of the burden of home work, and urged the wife to "retire late and rise early. Even though it takes her till midnight to do it, she should do what she has to do regardless of the difficulty of the undertaking. She should work until it is completed and be able to do it neatly."[6]

Both Mencius[7] and the *Li Ki*[8] emphasize the importance of spinning as an essential part of women's work. The *Nu Lun Yu*[9] outline in detail her duty as manufacturer of cloth fabrics.

---

[1] Lady Tsao, *Nu Chieh*, Chap. I.   Translated by I. T. Headland.
[2] *Ibid.*
[3] Jen Hsiao, *Nei Hsun*, Chap. I.   Translated by I. T. Headland.
[4] *Ibid.*, Chap. VII.
[5] *Li Ki*, Part XII, Book X, Sec. I.   Translated by J. Legge.
[6] Lady Tsao, *Nu Chieh*, Chap. I.
[7] Mencius, Book III, Chap. III, Part II.   (See Book IV)
[8] *Li Ki*, Book X, Sec. II: 36.
[9] Sung Jo Chao, *Nu Lun Yu*, Chap. II.

To woman was also given the task of making and preparing food for her family. The *Li Ki* mentions the meats, soups, vegetables, delicacies and fruits to be used in formal dinners and sacrifices. It also gives recipes for eight delicacies for the aged, involving painstaking and skillful preparation of materials with the crudest of equipment.[1]

Although minute ceremonials which typify and embody the duty of children to parents are described in the classics, little is said regarding the duty of parents to children. Filial piety exalts the mother to a place as queen among her children. In the books by women, however, there is some mention of the duties of a mother. "Woman's . . . instruction . . . is confined to her children,"[2] writes Jen Hsiao. "The rule of her instruction is to guide them with virtue and with moral rectitude, to educate them with modesty and humility, to lead them with diligence and economy; to do it with tenderness and love; to watch over them with sternness and faithfulness, thus will she establish their bodies and develop their virtue."[3] "As stately trees are stiff and the branches are not contiguous, as the abyss is clear and the fish do not hide in it, or as the sweet gourd clings to the drooping trees and as many grasses grow in the deep, moist valley, so children will be obedient to a tender and benevolent mother. This is a certain rule. . . . There are those who substitute indulgence for tenderness, blind love for virtue. This will spoil their children. That which does not swerve from what is proper, but diligently instructs the child is said to be tenderness."[4]

Perhaps the duty that lifted women higher than any other was the duty of assisting her husband at the sacrifices.[5]

Jen Hsiao says: "The husband and wife should together offer sacrifices. . . . The empress takes the lead in offering sacrifices to the spirits. She is the foundation of the empire. She prepares cleanly for the autumn and winter sacrifices, assists the emperor in the offering. . . . She stands in the temple

---

[1] *Li Ki*, Book X, Sec. II: 6. Translated by J. Legge.

[2] Mr. T. H. Cheng has reported the existence of dame schools in villages in the province of Chekiang. They taught reading and writing and some arithmetic.

[3] Jen Hsiao, *Nei Hsun*, Chap. XVI. Translated by I. T. Headland.

[4] *Ibid.*, Chap. XVIII.

[5] Cf. Book of Odes, Part I, Book II, Ode II, Part I, Book II, Ode IV.

early and late without thinking of weariness."[1]   The privilege of
sacrifice at the ancestral tablets was a foregleam of the permanent honor of wife and mother.   After death her spirit was wor-
shipped by her descendants.[2]

The standards of cultural education for Chinese women were
also well defined.   Music and correct conversation were enjoined,
and by women themselves, a need for knowledge of books was
recognized.   The Odes speak of a "beautiful, virtuous lady"
who "can respond to you in songs."[3]   Every boy in China who
has studied a year in school has learned these lines from his *San
Tze Ching:*[4]

> Tsae Wan Ke could play upon stringed instruments
> Seay Tao Wan likewise could sing and chant.
> These two though girls were intelligent and well informed
> You, then, my lads, should surely rouse to diligence![5]

In conversation rules were given that "females should not be
forward and garrulous, but observe strictly what is correct,
whether in suggesting advice to her husband, in remonstrating
with him, or in teaching her children; in maintaining etiquette,
humbly imparting her experience or in averting misfortune."[6]
The *Nu Chieh* sets this standard: "Choose your words, then
speak.   Of course, you will speak no bad words.   Let your words
be in season, then you will not bore others.   This may be said
to be the rule for women's conversation."[7]

The expressed desire for a broader education in books shows
very plainly that in spite of their modest compliance with the
duties placed upon them by society at least some women wished

---

[1] Jen Hsiao, *Nei Hsun*, Chap. XV.   Cf. W. Goodsell, *The Family*, p. 80.
This was a marked contrast to the place of woman in the Greek family where
sacrifice was performed only by the father.

[2] Cf. Book of Odes (*She King*), Part IV, Book I, Ode IV.   Translated by
J. Legge.   *Ibid.*, Ode VII.

[3] *Ibid.*, Part I, Book XII, Ode IV.

[4] *San Tze Ching:* "An epitome of all knowledge" which "every Chinese who
has learned to read knows by heart."   P. W. Kuo, *The Chinese System of
Public Education*, p. 53.

[5] *San Tze King*, line 158.   Translated in the *Chinese Repository*, Vol. IV,
p. 110.

[6] Lu Chow, *Nu Heo*, preface.   Translated in the *Chinese Repository*, Vol.
IX, p. 544.

[7] Lady Tsao, *Nu Chieh*, Chap. IV.   Translated by I. T. Headland.

for a higher and more wide-reaching standard for their education. "Examine now the superior men: They simply know the wife ought to be governed and the dignity of the household preserved. They, therefore, seek such books as will instruct the boys. It is not that the girls do not know that they ought to serve their husbands and that the rules of propriety ought to be preserved; but the boys have been instructed and the girls have not. Is not that placing too low an estimate on the relationship of the sexes? According to the ancient rules, when boys were eight years old, they began to read books and at fifteen they began to study. Ought not girls to do likewise?"[1] " 'A man's virtue is his ability.' This saying is nearly true. 'A woman's lack of ability is her virtue.' These words are false. Probably they did not know that the basis of ability and virtue is intimately related to the discussion of good and evil. Virtue promotes ability and ability completes virtue. . . . The superior man should instruct his sons, should he not also instruct his daughter?"[2]

The standards of conduct toward members of the family, of skill in home-keeping and garment making or cutting, in music, conversation, and literature, were directly taught in the home by educated parents and governesses, with especial attention before marriage.[3] Lady Tsao modestly gives her father gratitude for instruction, "Ignorant and stupid my mind was never quick of perception, though I had the good fortune to receive the special favor of my father."[4] Jen Hsiao, in the preface to the *Nei Hsun*, also bears witness to this custom, "In my youth, I received the instruction of my parents, having studied poetry and classical books, while at the same time I attended carefully my duties as a woman." Wang Chieh Fu, in the preface of her *Nu Fan Chieh Lu*, "In youth she was well versed in literature." In addition, "Her governess taught her the arts of pleasing speech and manners, to be docile and obedient."[5]

The classics portray the custom of tutelage just before marriage:

---

[1] Lady Tsao, *Nu Chieh*, Chap. IV. Translated by I. T. Headland.

[2] Wang Chieh Fu, *Nu Fan Chieh Lu*, Chap. X. Translated by I. T. Headland.

[3] Cf. Goodsell, *The Family*, p. 44.

[4] Lady Tsao, *Nu Chieh*, preface.

[5] *Li Ki*, Book X, Sec. II: 36. Translated by J. Legge.

"Anciently for three months before the marriage of a young lady
. . . she was taught the virtue, the speech, the carriage
and the work of a wife. When the teaching was accomplished,
she offered a sacrifice (to the ancestor) using fish for the victim
and soups made of duck-weed and pond-weed. So was she
trained to the obedience of a wife."[1] "At the marriage of a
young woman, her mother admonishes her, accompanying her to
the door on her leaving and cautioning her. . . . "[2]

The foregoing ideal of education for women is probably an important reason why the great majority of Chinese women remained in obscurity. Su Tung Pao, in *The Encyclopedia* says:
"Even with superior ability and extraordinary character they
(women) were not known in the world. Women who have intellectual, executive qualities cannot utilize these gifts, and those
with ability in the use of esthetic words are not known to others.
Then there are many who are good, kind-hearted and virtuous
and yet are unrewarded."[3] Professor S. L. Kiang says: "The
very fortunate learned something of (books). The middle class
girls learned to read only the *San Tzu Ching* (the Three Character Classics), the *Pai Chia Hsin* (Hundred Family Names) and
the *Nu Sze Hsu* (Four Classics for Girls).[4] In the low classes,
comprising 70 per cent or more of all the women in China, they
were not even taught to read their own family names. . . .
It is not to be wondered at, then, that since the Sung time (420
A.D.), there has been a proverb, believed implicitly to be as true
as the golden rule, 'A woman without ability is normal.' "[5]

However, to assume that women had no part in public life in
China would be untrue. Even in Chinese history where there
was no avowed purpose to preserve adequately the contributions
of womankind, the records abound with references to great women
and their deeds. There have been empress dowagers, who, rising from comparative obscurity, have seized the power of the
kingdom and have ruled people, officials and palace with severe

---

[1] *Li Ki*, Book XLI: 10. Translated by J. Legge.
[2] Mencius, Part II, Book III, Chap. II. Translated by J. Legge.
[3] *The Encyclopedia*, Vol. XXI, p. 18–19. Translated from the original
with the aid of Mr. T. H. Cheng.
[4] Cf. p. 7.
[5] Kiang, S. C., *Woman and Education in China*.

efficiency.[1] Other women, consorts of the emperors, have absorbed the attention of their masters and have caused the downfall of dynasties.[2] Still others have aided their husbands in ruling, and have wisely advised in matters of state.[3]

In addition to historical references, many books have been written with the specific aim of preserving for posterity the memory of wonderful women. The first books were written by Lu Hsiang[4] (approximately 80 B.C.). The qualities for which women were celebrated are not in every case those which are admired by the Occident, for they emphasize social rather than political abilities. The Biographies of Eminent Women (*Lieh Nu Chuan*) include 19 examples of women who were far-sighted and benevolent; 19 who were celebrated because of chastity; 18 who refused to marry after widowed whether by the death of husband or betrothed; 18 who were celebrated for far-sightedness and widowhood; 18 who should be considered as warnings for girls; 16 who were great mothers; and 16 who were celebrated for their docility and constancy.[5] Later (684 A.D.) Wang Chieh Fu included in her Short Records of Exemplary Women (*Nu Fan Chieh Lu*) eighty-six short biographies of those who were great. Her classification followed closely that of Lu Hsiang, adding 15 examples of virtuous empresses, and 14 who were noted for filial piety. In the great encyclopedia *Ku Chin T'u Shu Chi Ch'eng*, published in 1726, which was designed by the Emperor K'ang Hsi, "to provide a comprehensive survey of all that was best in the literature of the past, dealing with every branch of knowledge,"[6] 376 volumes are devoted to the works and lives of women. The classification here is still broader, and devotes

[1] Lu Chieh (194 B.C.), Pott, F. L. H., *Sketch of Chinese History*, p. 38; Empress Wu (684 A.D.), Pott, F. L. H., *loc. cit.*, p. 64; J. Bashford, *China*, p. 588; Empress Tze Hsi (1861–1908 A.D.), Bashford, J. W., *loc. cit.*, pp. 312 ff.; Bland and Blackhouse, *China under the Empress Dowager*.

[2] Moh Hsi (1818 B.C.), Pott, F. L. H., *Sketch of Chinese History*, p. 16; Ta Chi (1154 B.C.), *ibid.*, p. 20, Pao Ssu(781 B.C.), *ibid.*, p. 25.

[3] Empress Kiang Hou (806 B.C.), Bashford, J. W., *loc. cit.*, p. 570; Empress, wife of T'ai Tsung (620 A.D.), *ibid*, pp. 585–6; Lady Ma (1370 A.D.), *ibid.*, p. 598.

[4] Giles, H. A., *History of Chinese Literature*, p. 92.

[5] Compiled from the Index of *Lieh Nu Chuan* and translated by T. H. Cheng.

[6] Giles, L., *Alphabetical Index to the Chinese Encyclopedia*, Introduction, p. 6.

five volumes to those who became generals and military leaders, ten to those celebrated for their beauty, and one to those who were skillful in embroidery, painting and music.[1]

Not only were books written about women, but women themselves have contributed to the upbuilding of Chinese literature. Paradoxical though it may seem, the Book of Odes (*She King*) includes, as an integral part of the nation's most sacred literature, at least ten poems written by women. Commentators[2] agree that in Part I, Book III, Odes II, III, IV, and V were written by Chwang Keang and, in the same book, Ode XIV was written by a daughter of the house of Wei who longed to revisit her home. Similarly, Odes I and X, in Book IV, Odes V and VII, in Book V, were written by Chinese ladies of the Inner Courts. In addition to those in the classics, Chinese literature abounds in poems written by women. Among these may be mentioned Lady P'an, whose "Autumn Fan"[3] is known by all students of Chinese literature. China's history is indebted to a woman, Lady Tsao (50–112 A.D.),[4] for its record of the Later Han Dynasty. She was also the author of Instruction for Women (*Nu Chieh*). Later, Sung Jo Chao[5] (785–805 A.D.) compiled the Analects for Women (*Nu Lun Yu*). Later (1404 A.D.) Jen Hsiao[6] wrote her Teaching of the Inner Courts (*Nei Hsun*). Wang Chieh Fu[7] (970–1127 A.D.) selected from the examples of ancient women those who should be imitated by the girls of her generation, in her *Short Records of Exemplary Women* (*Nu Fan Chieh Lu*). These four books comprise "The Four Classics for Girls." The *Ku Kwo Wen Chi*,[8] a group of twenty-six volumes, is perhaps the most pretentious work by women. It is a collection of Chinese literary productions which were written by three hundred and seventy-three women. Still other writings are scattered through history, letters, memorials, and the miscellaneous books of the country. They have become an integral part of the great Chi-

---

[1] Giles, L., *Alphabetical Index to the Chinese Encyclopedia*, Introduction, p. 6.

[2] Cf. Notes, Book of Odes (*She King*); also The Little Preface.

[3] Cf. Giles, H. A., *History of Chinese Literature*, p. 101.

[4] Faber, E., *The Famous Women of China*, p. 46.

[5] *Ibid.*, p. 13.

[6] *Ibid.*, p. 12.

[7] *Ibid.*, p. 13; Williams, S. W., *History of China*, p. 39; *Chinese Repository*, Vol. IV, p. 106.

[8] Faber, E., *The Famous Women of China*, p. 11.

nese literature and are not separated because they are the product of the work of women.

The standards of woman's conduct set in the classics cannot be accepted as a literal picture of actual womanhood either in ancient or in modern times. Miss Sophia H. Chen, of Vassar College, says: "There has always been a minority who received education. In certain families the tradition of well educated women is kept up: One would learn the art of painting, another that of penmanship, still another the art of poetry!"[1] To-day in almost every home of refinement a private school is held for the sons of the family. Here the daughters are often permitted to learn the classics with their brothers, memorizing the same works under the same teachers. Furthermore, native ability and power of personality have often triumphed over cramping tradition. Nevertheless, that the teachings of the classics have moulded social attitudes toward women is undeniable. To-day, in conservative Chinese homes, the women are enjoined to be filial daughters, obedient wives and submissive sisters. The mother-in-law is the guardian and absolute ruler, by whom punishment to unruly daughters-in-law is meted out. The husbands, while often kindly toward, and sometimes fearful of the displeasure of their wives, are at liberty to bring home concubines.[2] Parents still decide whether or not a daughter may be educated, almost invariably preferring the son in education. They arrange for her marriage[3] with little regard for her wishes. In many homes the daughter has not been outside the courtyard of her father's house, and rarely, save in the progressive centers, is a girl permitted alone upon the streets. The home is considered the only proper sphere for women, and the tasks of the home their only proper work. In many interior places the women and girls spin and weave for the family all the clothing from hats to shoes. Household management and care of children according to traditional rules, a long life of drudgery with a crown of honor and power in old age, is the lot of most women in China. The traditional ideals of education, held by the conservative classes, are an integral part of the situation to-day. Upon the foundation laid centuries ago will the new education for women be built.

---

[1] Personal letter to the writer, February 19, 1918.

[2] There is a growing movement among the progressive group, both men and women, to make this custom unlawful.

[3] This applies equally to sons.

CHAPTER II

THE MODERN MOVEMENT IN WOMEN'S EDUCATION

MISSION SCHOOLS

In 1842 the cities of Canton, Amoy, Foochow, Ningpo and Shanghai were opened to foreign trade as treaty ports.[1]   Thus it was made possible for missionaries to establish schools in the coast cities of Central and Southern China.   The ignorance and superstitution of the women deeply impressed these early pioneers.   Foot binding and killing of infant girls were prevalent. The people were eager for the education of sons, but the daughters of the common people were thought scarcely worthy of such attention.   However, in the face of apathy[2] and even of opposition, schools for girls were opened, first by the Protestant missionaries, followed soon after by the Catholic missionaries.   Miss Aldersey, a member of the Church of England, was the pioneer of women's education.   At Ningpo in 1844 she opened the first school for Chinese girls, and supported it from her own income.[3]   In 1847[4] the Presbyterian Mission (which had founded its station in 1845[5]) started in this city another girls' school with two pupils.   The movement quickly spread to the other cities, and representatives opened schools: Mrs. Bridgeman in Shanghai under the American Board in 1849;[6] Mrs. Maclay in Foochow under the Meth-

---

[1] See Pott, F. L. H., *Sketch of Chinese History*, pp. 138–139.

[2] "A lady connected with the Chinese Mission" writes in 1855, "in the girls' day school I found fourteen scholars.   . . .   The old lady (teacher) reminded me that girls in the country were very stupid and dull; but that they would learn by and by.   She told me they were unwilling to attend without receiving some cash, because they thought it necessary to do some work every day to earn rice.   So I told her   . . .   that each pupil was to have 20 cash (or 1¼ cents) per day.   'Oh, then,' she replied, 'they will be eager to study.' " *The Spirit of Missions*, July, 1855, p. 319.

[3] See Burton, M., *Education of Women in China*, p. 35; Dean, *The China Mission*, p. 141; Presbyterian Mission Report, 1858, p. 87.

[4] Report, Presbyterian Board of Foreign Missions, 1847, p. 32.

[5] *Ibid.*, 1845, p. 22.

[6] Report, American Board of Foreign Com., 1849, p. 165.

odist Mission in 1851;[1] the Episcopal Mission in Shanghai in 1852;[2] the American Board in Foochow in 1853;[3] the Presbyterian Board in Canton in 1853;[4] the American Board in Canton in 1854;[5] the Presbyterian Board in Shanghai in 1857;[6] the Baptist Board at Ningpo in 1858;[7] the Wesleyan Church at Canton,[8] and the Reformed Church at Amoy[9] in 1860.

In 1858 a treaty with the American, English, and French governments gave to Protestant and Catholic missionaries official permission to propagate their faiths in any part of the country.[10] This opened the whole of China to mission work. For six years public opinion thwarted all efforts towards girls' schools in North China,[11] but finally, in 1864, seven girls in Tientsin, and five girls in Peking entered American Board schools.[12] In 1872, thirteen girls entered the Presbyterian Mission at Chefoo.[13] The pioneer school of Central China was founded in Kiukiang by the Methodist Mission in 1873. Gradually at first and then in rapid succession girls' schools under the missions have been opened, until to-day they are found in many cities. A large proportion of these are founded by American and British societies, but Norway, Sweden, Germany, and Switzerland are also represented.[14]

The course of study in these schools followed the contemporary studies in the West.[15] The Report of the Presbyterian School in Ningpo for 1849 gives the following schedule of studies: "The girls are taught to read their own language. They do not learn

---

[1] Report, Methodist Board of Foreign Missions, 1851, p. 134.

[2] *The Spirit of Missions*, November, 1852, p. 408.

[3] Report, American Board of Foreign Com., 1853, p. 132.

[4] Report, Presbyterian Board of Foreign Missions, 1854, p. 48

[5] Report, American Board of Foreign Com., 1854, p. 139.

[6] Report, Presbyterian Board of Foreign Missions, 1857, p. 71.

[7] Report, American Baptist Mission Union, 1860, p. 65.

[8] Wesleyan Report, 1860, p. 40.

[9] Reformed Church Report of Foreign Missions, 1860, p. 20.

[10] See Pott, F. L. H., *Sketch of Chinese History*, p. 155. Original text of treaty in Methodist Missions Report, 1859, p. 23.

[11] Report, American Board of Foreign Missions, 1864, p. 129.

[12] *Ibid.*, 1865, p. 126.

[13] Report, Presbyterian Board of Foreign Missions, 1872, p. 85.

[14] Cf. *China Mission Year Book*, 1917.

[15] The Report of the School Committee of Brighton, Mass., 1849–50, p. 19, speaks of the following subjects examined in District III: Reading, Geography, Arithmetic, oral and written, Philosophy, Dialogues and Singing.

the Chinese classics but study books containing Christian instruction, and some elementary books in science. They are taught Scriptural history orally by means of questions and answers. Arithmetic and geography form a part of their studies, and two of the girls are learning English. They are trained to habits of industry, and taught in such kinds of work as will fit them for usefulness in the stations they may occupy in future life."[1] The school in Foochow included in its courses of study "Christian morals and doctrine, geography, history, astronomy, mathematics, and daily reading of the Bible; also needlework and domestic economy."[2] It was "expected that all graduates be able to make, wash, and mend their own clothes, to cook and take care of the house."[3]

Bible study was given especial emphasis in order to bring the girls more closely in touch with Christian doctrine and perchance to win them to a belief in Christianity. A mission school in Swatow characterizes its curriculum as "mainly scriptural, though the girls learn other things . . . which will be useful to them when they return home. . . . Two Methodist American brothers were present at the examination and were much pleased with the recitations, particularly that given by the older girls in the book of Romans, and went so far as to say that they could outdo some theological schools at home."[4]

Gradually political history of other nations as well as of China, English language, and the Chinese classics became a part of the curriculum. In 1883, the progressive Chinese demanded "new educational methods, 'including the study of English, the Chinese classics, music and other accomplishments' " so insistently in one of the missions of Southern China that it led to the introduction of these subjects.[5]

Some years later, English is spoken of as "somewhat of an experiment as taught in the school," but the widened course of study justified itself, for the girls showed progress. In addition, the study "broadened and strengthened their minds, and made

[1] Report, Presbyterian Board of Foreign Missions, 1849, p. 36.
[2] Report, Methodist Board of Foreign Missions, 1864, p. 25.
[3] *Ibid.*, 1864, p. 25.
[4] Report, Woman's Baptist Society, 1882, p. 78.
[5] Report, Women's Foreign Mission Society, Methodist Church, 1883, p. 24.

them freer in giving expression to the experience of their hearts."[1] Participation in household duties and industrial arts remained an integral part of the school progress. In Tungchow the girls spent from one until three o'clock every day at some hand-work. They knew "how to do some kinds of embroidery and to make tidies. All but four were able to spin. . . . A well-to-do church member . . . engaged to take all the thread made in exchange for cloth."[2] In Ningpo, "the girls did all the cleaning, washing and cooking . . . to help the mission in its time of difficulty."[3]

During the past twenty years the curriculum has been changed as the curriculum of the West has been changed. Physical culture, general reading, elementary science, hygiene and domestic science have been included. The present course of study of the Central China Christian Educational Association requires for the lower primary school courses in Scripture, Chinese classics, Chinese language, history, geography, elementary science, object lessons, with English optional; for the higher primary schools, courses in Scripture, Chinese classics, Chinese language, history, geography, science (science readers and physiology), mathematics, English; for the middle schools, Scripture, Chinese classics, Chinese composition, history, geography, zoölogy, botany, physics, chemistry, mathematics (algebra, geometry, trigonometry) with psychology as an alternative, and English.[4] The Keen School (Chung Hsi) of Tientsin thus outlines its program for advance: "We (desire to) see every girl who graduates from Keen School in the future going out with something she can teach others, and by which she might earn her own livelihood if necessary. (This . . . calls) for normal training and practice work, including places for day school, kindergarten, industrial work and domestic science."[5]

Mission schools of all Protestant churches and all grades are united under the Chinese Christian Educational Association[6] with an advisory council made up of members from eight geo-

---

[1] Report, Women's Foreign Mission Society Methodist Church, 1886, p. 30.
[2] *Woman's Work for Woman*, January, 1877, p. 372.
[3] Report, Presbyterian Board of Foreign Missions, 1899, p. 43.
[4] *The Educational Review*, July, 1916.
[5] Report, North China Woman's Conference (Methodist), 1917, p. 9.
[6] *China Mission Year Book*, 1907, p. 378.

graphical districts. The central association discusses questions of wide significance, and formulates plans for educational progress. Affiliated associations in Fukien, Kwangtung, Shantung and Honan, Manchuria, Chili and Shansi, Hunan, West, Central and East China[1] adapt and put into execution the suggestions of the general committee, and propose further problems for consideration. Each association has adopted a course of study to be the standard for its district, and honors of some kind are given to those schools which reach the standard set. Uniform examinations are being introduced in several systems, and in the West China Union two executive officers give full time to supervision and administration. Membership in these associations is voluntary. No distinction is made between girls' and boys' schools. The system of girls' education as outlined by the missionary union may be illustrated by Figure 1.

Lower primary schools are scattered through the villages near the larger centers. These are usually day schools, although lower primary, higher primary, and middle schools are often incorporated into one so-called "boarding school." The dividing line in the primary schools is not uniform in the various associations. Some divide the course into three years for the lower primary schools and four years for the higher primary schools. The middle school endeavors to prepare girls both for teaching and for college through elective courses. In addition, many centers have established special schools for the training of teachers. There are four centers where instruction of college grade is given to women: North China Woman's College, a union institution at Pekin; Ginling College, a union institution at Nanking; Foochow Woman's College and the American Board College in Foochow; Canton Christian College in Canton, and the Church Missionary Society in Fukien. The total attendance at these colleges in 1916 was sixty-four girls.[2] A Union medical school in Peking and denominational centers in other cities prepare women to become physicians. A large proportion of the hospitals train women nurses.

The influence of girls' mission schools in China, both in preparing teachers and in bringing about a social demand for women's education, has been exceedingly strong. Teachers in

---

[1] Gamewell, F. D., Report in *Educational Review*, July, 1915.

[2] See *China Mission Year Book*, 1917.

the missions are recruited as far as possible from their own graduates, and many of the teachers in government institutions for girls have been trained in the missions.   Mr. P. W. Kuo says: "Perhaps the earliest source of obtaining teachers capable in a

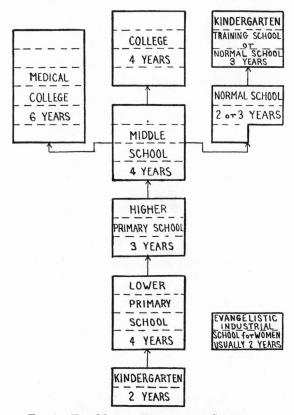

Fig. 1.   The Mission Educational System.

way to meet the new demand was the missionary schools.   . . . Some of the better and higher institutions managed by missionaries turned out many graduates more or less fitted to assume the responsibility of teaching in new schools.   It is but natural that they were sought for by the government as well as by private schools."[1]

---

[1] P. W. Kuo, *Training of Teachers in China*, pp. 19–20.   (Master's thesis, Teachers College, 1912.

3

The mission schools have also helped to overcome the prejudice toward education of girls and are now doing what they can to meet the popular demand for increased opportunities. Mrs. Ashmore, after about fifteen years of service, gives her experience: "when I first took the school we were obliged to tease the parents for the privilege of educating their girls. Now I am continually asked, 'Is there any room in the schools for my girls?' They know they must make application before school opens in order to get them in."[1] "Said an old native preacher who was listening to the examination (of the Foochow Girls' School), 'According to this, our girls ought to eat thĕ rice grains, and our boys, the rice water.'"[2] "Perhaps the most remarkable change is that with respect to the education of women and girls," writes Bishop Huntington. "Our own schools are utterly inadequate to meet the growing demands. The girls' academy at Hengchow (an interior city of Hunan) reports attendance larger than the building could comfortably accommodate. Were we ready to receive them, three times our number would be glad to attend."[3]

The growth in the number of girls in Protestant mission schools in China may be seen from the following table:

> In 1849,[4] 3 schools, probably fewer than 50 pupils
> In 1860,[5] 12 schools, approximately 196 pupils
> In 1869,[6] 31 schools, 556 pupils
> In 1877,[7] 38 schools, 524 pupils
> In 1896,[8] 308 schools, 6,798 pupils
> In 1910,[9] (no report available), 16,190 pupils
> In 1915,[10] 45,168 pupils
> In 1916,[11] 50,173 pupils

[1] Report, Woman's Baptist Missionary Society, 1898, p. 151.

[2] Report, W. F. M. S. of the Methodist Church, 1899, p. 42.

[3] Report, Protestant Episcopal Church, 1913, p. 213.

[4] Compiled from Presbyterian Report, 1849; American Board Foreign Mission Report, 1849.

[5] Compiled from Baptist Report, 1860; Presbyterian Report, 1860; American Board Report, 1860; Wesleyan Report, 1860. Checked by the reports of all other reports of missions in China at that time.

[6] *Chinese Recorder*, Vol. II, p. 61 (August, 1869).

[7] Compiled from Records of the Missionary Conference, May, 1877, p. 326.

[8] Compiled from *The China Mission Handbook*, 1896.

[9] Compiled from *The World Atlas of Christian Missions*, 1910.

[10] Compiled from *China Mission Year Book*, 1916.

[11] *Ibid.*, 1917.

The first sisters of the Catholic Church reached China on June 21, 1848.[1] They were the pioneers among those who have established work in many cities of the nation. Although school work has been only one phase of their service, it has been considered a very important activity. Rev. J. A. Walsh, president of Maryknoll, writes: "In my recent journey I found schools for girls in Tientsin, Peking, Chentingfu, Paotingfu, Hankow, Shanghai, Hongkong, Canton, and every other place I visited. Some of these schools were for somewhat advanced scholars, and were attended by daughters of well-to-do Chinese. Others were for children of the poor, and of such schools there are seemingly as many as there are missions."[2] The subjects taught in the lower schools are much like those in Protestant mission schools. Mrs. Little reports a visit to one of them: "The girls read (Chinese) fairly, and then sang. . . . They could not answer questions in arithmetic, but all had rosy cheeks, clean faces, and bright intelligent eyes."[3] The subjects outlined for the Canton school, which may be considered typical, are: "English, French, music, drawing, the usual grammar and high school branches and most important of all, Catholic doctrine, principles and practice."[4]

In 1912 the enrollment of girls in the higher schools was 1453, in the lower schools, 48,534,[5] making a total of 49,987 girls in Catholic schools.

PRIVATE SCHOOLS

In 1897 the first school for girls, established and financed by the Chinese people, was opened. Mr. King Ling Shan, together with other leading men of Shanghai, resolved at their first meeting that "as gentlemen they could finance the scheme, but that the executive management should be entrusted to their wives. Accordingly, in due time a committee of ladies undertook the further management of the enterprise."[6] The school opened with an enrollment of sixteen on June first. In 1898 a day school

---

[1] *Catholic Missions*, April, 1913, p. 57. See Streit, P. C., *Atlas Hierarchicus*. p. 42.

[2] Rev. J. A. Walsh, personal letter, April 26, 1918.

[3] Mrs. A. Little, *In the Land of the Blue Gown*, p. 123.

[4] *Catholic Missions*, May, 1910, p. 76.

[5] *Zeitschrift für Missions-Wissenschaft*, 1912, p. 212.

[6] Triennial Report of the China Educational Association, 1899, p. 160.

in another part of the city was added. In May, 1899, there were thirty-five girls in the older school and twenty girls in the new day school. They taught English, Chinese books, drawing, painting, geography, arithmetic, and foreign sewing. A reaction which was preliminary to the Boxer uprising closed this school in 1899.[1] As soon as the anti-Western furor had subsided, in 1901 a changed Empress Dowager issued an edict[2] permitting the opening of girls' schools. Slowly at first, then, as they succeeded and met with no governmental antagonism, more rapidly, schools were opened. The following table shows the growth of the movement in Shanghai:

> 1901—Wu Pen School (Strive for Duty)
> 1902—I Kwo School (Love for Country)
> 1903—Chung Mang School (Worship the Noble)
> 1904—Ch'eng Tung School (East of the City)
> 1905—Anglo Chinese School
>   T'ien Tsu Hwei (Natural Feet Society)
>   Chi Sin School (Cultivate Elegance)
>   Pei Hao School (Develop Goodness)
> 1906—Fu Chiang School (Help to Attain Strength)
>   Ching Hwa School (Struggle for Reform)
>   Tsai Nyi School (Silk Worm Industry)[3]

"In Tientsin in 1906 there were five girls' schools under government supervision with an aggregate attendance of about 250 women and girls."[4] In Peking the Manchu princesses opened several schools for girls which set an example that common people might follow without fear.[5]

The private schools have since then flourished in every part of China. After the Revolution in 1911, an even greater impetus was given to woman's education, and many wealthy citizens founded girls' schools as an evidence of their patriotism. A widow of Hangchow, Chekiang Province, opened a school with funds subscribed by officials and progressive citizens. The school flourished the first year, but the second year her request for

---

[1] *Chinese Recorder*, October, 1899, p. 500.

[2] Headland, I. T., *Court Life in China*, p. 103.

[3] See Paddock, Estelle, article in *Woman's Work in the Far East*, June, 1907, p. 79.

[4] See Mrs. M. L. Taft's article in *Woman's Work in the Far East*, September, 1906, p. 105.

[5] Headland, I. T., *Court Life in China*, Chap. XIV.

funds did not meet with ready response. After a desperate effort
she wrote to the officials saying, "When these letters reach you,
I will be a corpse, as I propose to take my own life in order to
arouse public sentiment to the importance of the education of
girls." This brought about the desired result, for memorial
funds were quickly raised to perpetuate the work of this martyr
to the cause of woman's education.[1]

One of the most interesting of the schools founded at this time
was the Ching Tsun School in Tientsin, managed entirely by
some of the graduates of the Girls' Normal School. "It was
started by a group of these girls just before they graduated last
summer (1912). It is now (1913) directed by six or seven of
them who do all the teaching . . . and give their services
free. Two live at the school and spend their whole time there,
but the rest are teaching elsewhere as well, and only give a few
hours per week to . . . Ching Tsun. . . . Each of the
girls . . . gave her first month's salary to support this school.
It is now kept up in part by these funds, but gets a grant
of $60.00 (Mexican) per month from the local educational au-
thorities, which covers rent. The furniture is old stock . . .
from the Normal School. Scholars pay one dollar (Mexican)
per month . . . which goes toward food for the teachers
who live at the school, together with servants' wages, etc. In
December there were over 50 scholars; 14 in the senior class and
over 30 in the lower class, whose ages ranged from 5 or 6 to 15 or
16 years. The fact that the total number of scholars has now
reached 98 with 23 in the senior class and 75 in the junior speaks
well for the good management and popularity of the school."[2]

A great impetus has been given to industrial training for girls
through these institutions. "The Cheng Tung School of Shanghai offers an extension course in practical arts, including satchel
making, embroidery, lace work, pasteboard work and drawing."[3]
"At Nantung, Mr. Chang established a school for girls . . .
with courses in silk culture, raising silkworms, unravelling cocoons, spinning, tailoring, cooking, weaving rushes, artificial

---

[1] See *Cyclopedia of Education*, "China, Recent Educational Reform," Vol. I,
p. 638.

[2] Saxelby, E. Mary, *Woman's Work in Tientsin*, April, 1913, pamphlet.

[3] Translated from *Chinese Educational Review*, 1909, with aid of T. H.
Cheng, "Shih Chuan," p. 45.

flower making."[1] In Changsha a special school for embroidery was started.[2] In Hsiang Twan there are four special courses: Sewing, silkworm rearing, dyeing, and crocheting.[3] Some of these schools open their doors, only to fail, but the courses they offer grow out of the needs of the people. There is an expressed desire for education for women that will give definite, measurable results in a short time.

The private schools include all grades, and every degree of efficiency from that one which taught English from A to L,[4] to the Chu Nan Girls' Normal School, equipped with garden, infirmary and gymnasium, offering normal, higher, and lower elementary courses and reporting in 1916 a total enrollment of 301.[5] Many of these schools have become incorporated as government schools.

GOVERNMENT SCHOOLS

In 1901 the edict of the Empress Dowager Tze Hsi permitted the establishment of girls' schools in China. The immediate response in the numbers of private schools revealed the desire of the people for such education. However, not until 1907[6] were schools for girls definitely and officially provided for by the government. Then a system of education was outlined similar to that planned for boys' schools in 1903. When the educational laws for the Republic were drawn up in 1912, the Minister of Education issued this most important order: "The firmness of the foundation upon which the Republic of China has been founded depends on Education. Under the new form of government the responsibilities of the officials and private individuals who are engaged in educational work are greater and heavier than ever before. The backwardness of our country, that has hindered China from competing with the World Powers, is not

---

[1] Translated from *Chinese Educational Review*, May 25, 1912, with aid of Mr. T. H. Cheng, "Shih Chuan."

[2] *Ibid.*, September 10, 1910. "Shih Chuan," p. 80.

[3] *Ibid*, 1916.

[4] Mrs. Gamewell, *Gateway to China*, p. 121.

[5] Translated from the *Chinese Educational Review*, 1916, with the aid of Mr. T. H. Cheng.

[6] Kuo, P. W., *Chinese System of Public Education*, pp. 78, 101, 104.

due to the stupidity or laziness of its people, but is due to lack of education. We must, hereafter, make our best effort to develop and encourage women's education as well as that for men. We must emphasize and provide for social as well as for school education."[1]

To make the education of girls more possible, the Board of Education decreed on May 11, 1912, that "In the lower elementary grades, boys and girls may attend the same school."[2] The boys and girls in higher primary schools, however, are required to form separate classes.[3]

Soon followed the order that definitely established the ideal of universal education and the aim of the minimum length for school life. The law makes no distinction between girls and boys. "Every child, after the second day of its sixth year of age, should enter primary school until fourteen years of age. Children below six years of age cannot be forced to attend school."[4] The present regulation for universal education characterizes the ages from six to fourteen as the "learning years" of each child. Parents and guardians are responsible for the failure of their children to attend schools during this period, and must report sickness or poverty to the authorities. This regulation is fortified by a child labor law which prohibits employment of children of school age.

The Chinese educational system as outlined September 3, 1912, provides as its foundation the four-year coeducational primary school, called Citizens' School since July 31, 1915. This school prepares for three alternative schools: higher primary school, with a course of three years; vocational school "A" of three years; and a supplementary school of two years. The higher primary school prepares for four schools: middle school, with a course of four years; vocational school "B," with a course of three years; supplementary school, with a course of two years;

---

[1] An order issued September 2, 1912, by the Minister of the Board of Education, translated by Mr. J. T. Hsi, from Educational Documents (*Chiao Yu Pu Wen Tu Liao Piang*), Chap. V, p. 23: art. 21–22.

[2] *Ibid.*

[3] Orders issued by the Board of Education on the Regulations for Higher Primary Schools (*Chiao Yu Pu Ching Chun Kao Teng Hsiao Hsueh Hsiao Ling*), art. 16. Translated by Mr. J. T. Hsi.

[4] An order issued by the Board of Education, September 28, 1912. Translated by Mr. J. T. Hsi from Educational Documents (*Chiao Yu Pu Ling*), p. 16.

and normal school with a course of five years. The middle school prepared for college with six or seven years' course and technical school with a four or five years' course, and the higher normal school with a five years' course. The lower normal school graduates may finish the higher normal in three years. The Chiao Pu illustrated the system as in Figure 2.

In 1913 for the education of girls there were:

2482 Primary Schools	100 Lower Normal Schools
446 Higher Primary Schools	1 Higher Agricultural School
2 Agricultural Schools	3 Higher Industrial Schools
53 Industrial Schools	15 Higher Special Schools
11 Special Schools	1 Higher Normal School[1]
11 Middle Schools	

The college and technical schools have yet to be added in order to make the educational system complete for women. Doubtless these will eventually be built.

The courses of study as suggested by the Board of Education in 1915 comprise for the Citizens' School: the Chinese classics, Chinese literature, ethics, mathematics, manual training, drawing, music, and physical training. Sewing is added to the curriculum for girls' schools.[2] "The courses in the citizens' schools on ethics, classics, Chinese literature and mathematics are required. The rest of the courses may be excused on account of the physical incapacity of the pupils."[3] The general aim of the Citizens' School is "to train students both physically and mentally with proper emphasis upon morality, because ethics is the foundation for citizenship. The students should also obtain a foundation of that education which is essential to everyday life."[4]

The course of study prescribed for the Higher Primary Schools consists of ethics, classics, language, mathematics, history, geography, science, agriculture, commercial courses, modern language, domestic science, manual training, drawing, singing and

---

[1] From the Annual Report of the Board of Education 1913 (*Chung Hwa Min Kwoa Ti Er Tze Chiao Yu T'ung Chi Tu Piao*). Translated by Mr. J. T. Hsi, p. 1.

[2] Regulations for the Citizens' Schools (*Kwoa Min Hsueh Hsiao Ling*), issued July 31, 1915, art. 12.

[3] *Ibid.* Chap. III, art. 15.

[4] *Ibid.*, art. 1.

physical training.[1] "The object of history is to enable children
to comprehend the fundamental principles of the development of
China and to prepare for citizenship. The contents of history

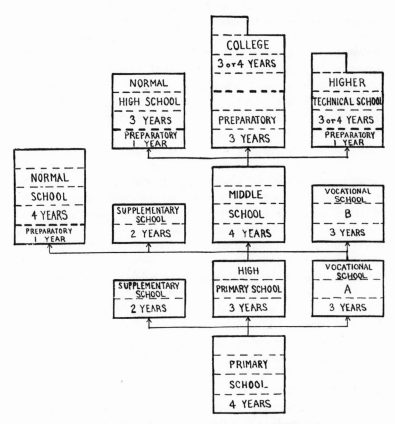

Fig. 2. The Government Educational System.

should treat of the achievements of Hwang Ti,[2] the biographies
of all great men, the development of civilization in the Far East,
the changes of the forms of government and the relations of our

---

[1] Order issued by Board of Education on the Regulations for Higher Primary
School, art. 2, 9.

[2] Hwang Ti (2697 b.c.) was one of the earliest traditional important rulers
of the Empire. He invented the Chinese Calendar and his wife taught Seri-
culture to the people. See Pott, F. L. H., *A Sketch of Chinese History*, p. 10.

country to other countries during the last one hundred years.[1]
. . . The object of geography is to teach students to know
the surface of the earth and the conditions under which men live.
It also teaches pupils the present conditions of their own country
and may develop patriotism. The geographical conditions of
their country, its climate, its capital, its commercial centers; the
movement of the earth and its effect on man, on commerce, on
products; the capitals of other countries, their commercial centers and their products should be taught. The political and
economic condition of China in relation to that of other countries should be included. In teaching geography the teacher
must use as a basis of comparison physical features of the locality.
This method will arouse interest and stimulate local pride.[2]
. . . The object of science is to teach students to know the
natural phenomena of things in relation to mankind. The
courses should consist of botany, zoölogy, mineralogy. These
courses should give familiarity with the appearance, names and
functions of natural objects, and should show the relation of their
development to human progress. The fundamental principles
of chemistry and physics, including analysis, synthesis and con-
struction of simple apparatus, and the principles of hygiene are
also to be taught. In science the courses offered must be practical. They must be related to agriculture, fishing industry, or
domestic science. Elementary experiments shall be required."[3]
" The object of teaching agriculture is that students may know the
principles of agriculture, that they may develop a habit of diligence, and that they may understand local conditions and possibilities in agriculture, forestry and fishing. Fertility of the soil,
possibility of irrigation, use of fertilizers and agricultural instru-
ments; the methods of farming, rearing silkworms, planting mul-
berry trees, raising cattle and other domestic animals. Any
details of the above mentioned courses may be chosen to suit the
local needs.[4] . . . The object of commercial courses is to
teach the principles of commerce. This study should also develop

---

[1] Order issued by Board of Education on the Regulations for Higher Primary Schools, Chap. I, art. 3.

[2] *Ibid.*, art. 4.

[3] *Ibid.*, art. 5.

[4] *Ibid.*, art. 6.

in students a habit of diligence and trustworthiness. Under commercial courses, trading, banking, transportation, insurance and other courses connected with commerce should be chosen so as to suit the local need. In teaching commercial courses, bookkeeping should be added to Chinese language, mathematics, geography and science.[1] The object of teaching modern language is to enable students to speak and use a foreign language. . . . In choosing text-books the teacher must select those appropriate to the student's age. In teaching modern language use practical words and in translation use pure language, such as Mandarin.[2] In teaching home administration the object is to train students to manage a home. Habits of economy and of cleanliness should be developed in them. Sewing and other fundamental principles of domestic science should be taught."[3]

"The courses of study for middle school are ethics, the Chinese classics, modern language, history, geography, mathematics, natural science, physics, chemistry, civics, economics, drawing, manual training, music, physical education. For girls, middle school courses on gardening, housekeeping and sewing are to be added. Of the modern languages, English should be emphasized, and French, German or Russian, is to be studied, according to the location of the place."[4]

The Normal School curriculum includes ethics, classics, education (psychology, logic, philosophy, history of education, educational administration, practice teaching), Chinese literature, penmanship, modern language, history, geography, mathematics, (arithmetic, algebra, geometry, trigonometry, bookkeeping, methods of teaching), natural science (botany, zoölogy, psychology, mineralogy, geology, methods of teaching), physics, chemistry, political science, drawing, manual training, domestic science and gardening, sewing, music and physical education. Although they are given comparatively few hours in the course of study, the domestic science courses, especially in the normal schools, are considered of highest importance. Mr. Tang Hwa Lung, Minis-

---

[1] Order issued by Board of Education on the Regulations for Higher Primary Schools, art. 7.

[2] *Ibid.*, art. 8.

[3] *Ibid.*, art. 9.

[4] Orders for Middle Schools given by the Board of Education, December 2, 1912 (*Chung Hsueh Hsiao Ling*), art. 1. Translated by Mr. J. T. Hsi.

ter of Education in 1914, writes: "We should study how to develop intellect and skill (in our school girls). Otherwise, it will be impossible for China to have a footing in the world of civilization."[1] However, "the policy of the Board is to make women good wives and mothers." In 1916, Mr. Chiang Han Chi, president of the Girls' Normal School in Hanchow, wrote: "The (conservative) conception of girls' education is responsible for our non-progress. . . . The girls in the normal schools should have some domestic education, but they cannot be absorbed in it. . . . Nevertheless . . . we must have good mothers and good housewives."[2] In the domestic science department of Normal School Number I of Kiangsu Province, a practice home of three rooms, appropriately equipped, is used for experiment. Every month three pupils above the third year class make it their home. With the permission of the parents they adopt a child from the elementary school to live with them. They change the arrangement of the furniture frequently and cook the suppers themselves. In the cookery department of the school sixteen girls participate daily, alternating the tasks. Two girls make the menus for the day, and these are systematically followed.[3]

The growth of the number of girls in school since 1904 can be readily shown from the following table:

In 1904, 25 schools,   468 pupils
    1905, 71 schools,   1,665 pupils
    1906, 233 schools,   5,945 pupils
    1907, 391 schools, 11,936 pupils[4]
    1908, 513 schools, 18,202 pupils
    1909, 722 schools, 26,465 pupils
    1910–11, no reports. Many schools closed because of the Revolution.
    1912, 2,389 schools, 141,130 pupils[5]
    1913, 3,123 schools, 166,964 pupils[6]
    1917, 3,533 schools, 170,789 pupils[7]

---

[1] *Chinese Educational Review*, 1914. Translated by T. H. Cheng.

[2] *The Chinese Weekly*, 1916. Translated by T. H. Cheng.

[3] *Chinese Educational Review*, 1916, Vol. VIII; No. VI. Translated by T. H. Cheng.

[4] The year girls' schools were made an integral part of the system.

[5] Statistics of the Department of Education of China, 1912 (*Chung Hwa Min Kwoa Ti Tse Chiao Yu Tung Chi Tu Piao*), p. 1.

(Notes [6] and [7] on page 35).

RELATIONSHIP BETWEEN MISSION, PRIVATE AND GOVERNMENT
SCHOOLS

Mission schools were the pioneers in the field of modern education and are to-day rendering great service in all departments of school work.   Private schools represented the first efforts of the Chinese people to provide for themselves the new type of schools, and are to-day a strong factor in educational progress.   The government schools, established in 1907, have accepted the new education from the West and have grown much more rapidly than either mission or private schools.   To-day, after only eleven years of existence, they comprise the largest educational system in China.

The government educational authorities, however, exercise no cramping control over either private or mission schools.   The private schools may sustain three relationships to the government.   If they receive no funds, they may be absolutely independent from all control and inspection (although periodical reports to the government authorities are required).   If subsidies from the government are received, in addition to reports they are inspected periodically by officials and are required to maintain a certain standard of work.   If there are no government schools near, private schools may be delegated by the government to provide education for children in the immediate vicinity, and are thus incorporated into the government system.

The relation of the mission schools to the government system is still undetermined.   The mission schools are given full freedom to extend education and courtesies are continually exchanged between government and mission institutions.   Officials and leaders in national affairs contribute, as individuals, to mission school support and educate their daughters in mission schools. Perhaps some mission centers report statistics of attendance to the provincial educational authorities, but it is not universally done.   Recently provincial commissioners have been instructed "to report on all the schools established by foreigners in their

---

[6] Statistics of the Department of Education of China, 1913.

[7] From a private report sent to the writer from the Minister of Education of China, March 5, 1918.   The Minister says in part, "Though it (the table) is made on the basis of recent statistics it is not quite accurate because many provincial girls' schools have not yet been reported to the Board of Education."

respective provinces."[1]   No official recognition, however, has yet been accorded to the missionary educational systems, although a basis of recognition which will leave freedom for change and experiment, worked out through conference with the Christian educational associations, would probably be welcomed. Such recognition would make possible national organization of plans for education which would eliminate competition and would thus utilize all available forces for the rapid promotion of education.   It is apparent that only united concentrated effort can bring any adequate opportunity for education to this generation of Chinese girlhood.

---

[1] *The Educational Review*, July, 1918, p. 269.

CHAPTER III

THE PRESENT SITUATION

THE RAPID RISE OF GIRLS' SCHOOLS

The outstanding feature in the education of women to-day is the rapid rise in the number of students. The growth began in 1877 during the period of missionary education, before the government permitted schools for women. This growth was contemporaneous with the first educational mission to America.[1] The numbers increased gradually until 1896. The Boxer outbreak of 1900 had no permanent detrimental effect on the enrollment in mission schools although there are no statistical reports for girls' schools until 1908. The agitation for reform and governmental encouragement from 1902–1907 resulted in the establishment of Chinese private, municipal and government institutions. The enrollment in these, together with that in missions schools, inceased steadily until the Revolution in 1910–11 made it necessary to suspend work in Chinese schools in many places. However, the most remarkable increase of the entire movement took place in 1912. The mission report of 1915 and the partial government report of 1917 indicate that the numbers continue to grow. The following table shows the statistical increase for all China, 1849–1915, mission schools only:[2]

In 1849, less than, 50 pupils
    1860, 196 pupils
    1869, 556 pupils
    1877, 524 pupils
    1896, 6,358 pupils
    1909, Government and
    1910, Mission, 42,655 pupils[3]
    1916, Mission and
    1917, Government, 220,705 pupils[4]

---

[1] Kuo, P. W., *Chinese System of Education*, p. 68.

[2] It has been possible to find records of the number of girls in school in Catholic Missions for the year 1912 only. Hence they are not included in this table.

[3] In 1909 was printed the last available report before the suspension of government schools during the Revolution. In 1910 was printed the first report of Mission Schools for girls after the Boxer Rebellion.

[4] These reports are the latest ones which are available.

ELIMINATION IN THE SCHOOLS AS A WHOLE

The great majority of the girls in school in China attend the lower elementary schools: 170,057 are in the lower primary or

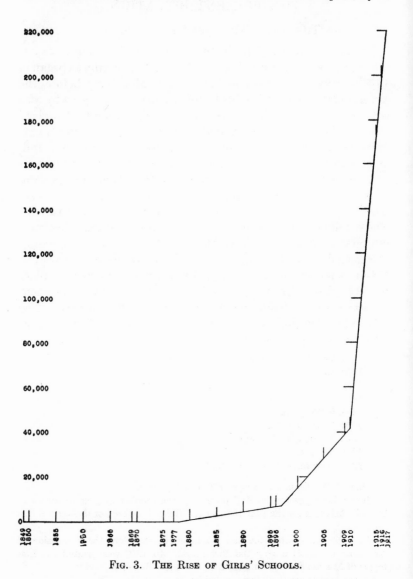

FIG. 3. THE RISE OF GIRLS' SCHOOLS.

citizens' schools; 27,909 are in higher primary schools,[1] and 14,909 in middle schools.

Lower Elementary	*Mission*[2]	*Government*[3]	*Total*
Lower Elementary or Special Schools	40,905	133,509	174,414
Higher Elementary	6,889	21,655	28,544
Middle or above Normal School	2,122	11,638	13,760

Over 80 per cent of the girls who enter school are in the lower elementary school, 13 per cent in the higher elementary school, and 6 per cent in the middle school. This indicates that eight out of ten girls who have enrolled in schools are in their first four years of study,[4] and that 6 per cent only have remained for seven years of study. When curricula are to be considered, this fact is of vital significance.

GEOGRAPHICAL DISTRIBUTION OF EDUCATIONAL INSTITUTIONS

The universal tendency of schools to center in the large cities and to neglect country districts is evident in China. The coast provinces are comparatively well provided with schools while the inland provinces have only a scattering few. A notable exception to this rule, however, is Szechuen, which leads the entire nation in the number of government schools and ranks third in the number of Protestant mission schools for girls. It was impossible to secure information concerning the location of government schools for girls, but the map of the location of Protestant mission schools for girls shows the general distribution (see frontispiece).

The number of girls' schools in each province is made clear in the following table:

Province	*Mission Schools*[5]	*Government Schools*[6]	*Total*
Anhwei	85	25	110
Chekiang	182	249	431

---

[1] *China Mission Year Book*, 1917, statistics for 1916.

[2] This includes only Protestant missions. Catholic statistics are not available.

[3] Annual Report of the Board of Education.

[4] This high percentage may be partially explained by the growth in the number of girls in schools, since, of course, all girls must begin in the lower elementary grades.

[5] Committee on Education of the Edinburgh Commission on Education.

[6] Report of Minister of Education, 1913, p. 1.

Province	Mission Schools	Government Schools	Total
Chili	141	324	465
Peking		68	
Fukien	650	19	669
Honan	73	83	156
Hunan	88	131	219
Hupeh	236	194	430
Kansu	10	9	19
Kiangsi	46	69	115
Kiangsu	244	263	507
Kwangsi	20	64	84
Kweichow	25	114	139
Kwangtung	481	51	532
Shansi	84	259	343
Shangtung	780	197	977
Shensi	24	68	92
Szechuen	474	340	816
Yunnan	54	252	306

The coast provinces of Chili, Shangtung, Kiangsu, Chekiang, Fukien and Kwangtung aggregate 3,581 schools. The central provinces, bordering on the trade routes: The Yantze River and the railroads; Szechuen, Hupeh, Hunan, Kiangsi, Anhwei, and Honan, aggregate 1,845 schools. The inland provinces of Yunnan, Kweichow, Kwangsi, Kansu, Shensi and Shansi report only 983 schools for girls. Thus, as a rule, trade and schools have developed together, leaving as yet untouched, great geographical sections of the country. The comparatively strong hold of tradition upon those who live in country districts, the large percentage of rural population, and the primitive methods of transportation accentuate the difficulty of this problem.

Number of Girls in School Compared with Total Number of Girls of School Age

In 1910, the Ministry of the Interior (*Minchengpu*) reported to the United States Department of State a population of 331,188,-000.[1] In *Some Problems in Administration*, Dr. G. D. Strayer places the proportion of school children to the total population of the United States at 17.4 per cent. Assuming that the same proportion will be approximately correct for China, there are

---

[1] See Bashford, J. W., *loc. cit.*, p. 19.

probably in that republic to-day about 56,626,712 children of school age. Half of these, or 28,313,356, are probably girls.

In 1916, Protestant missions reported 49,916 girls in school; in 1912 the Catholic mission reported 49,987 girls in school; in 1918 the government reported 170,789 girls in private and government schools. Thus, from the latest statistics available of the three great branches of education, there is a total of 270,692 girls in school.[1] The number of girls who probably do not yet attend school is 28,042,412. The proportion of girls not in school is 95 per cent of the girls of school age. This is graphically shown as follows:

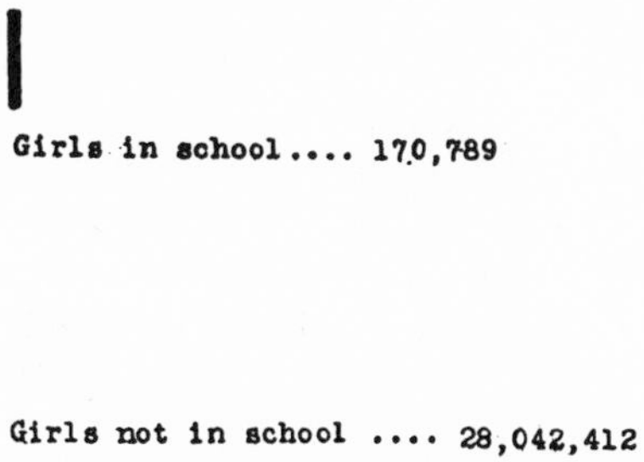

|

Girls in school 170,789

Girls not in school 28,042,412

FIG. 4. SCHOOL POPULATION OF GIRLS OF SCHOOL AGE.

It is evident, therefore, that the number of girls attending school in China is increasing rapidly and that the schools are clustered in the great cities along trade routes. Probably not one out of one hundred girls of school age enters an educational institution, and four-fifths of those who do enter are registered in the first three years of the course. Over twenty-eight million girls of school age do not yet attend school. Education for girls in China has, in reality, barely commenced.

---

[1] Statistics for boys' schools from the same sources at the same times are:

Catholic missions	82,863	(*Zeitschrift für Missions-Wissenschaft*, 1912)
Government missions	3,476,242	(Government Report, 1913)
Protestant missions	117,483	(*Mission Year Book*, 1917)
Estimated total number of boys in school	3,676,588	

PART II

CHAPTER I

THE SCOPE OF THE INVESTIGATION

In order to study the actual status and the practical results of the present education of women in China, questionnaires were sent to eighteen widely distributed centers. Fourteen of these were under mission control, and four under governmental control. The questionnaires were prepared for individual replies, and hence were necessarily in the Chinese language. A separate list of questions was formulated for each of the following groups: pupils, teachers, graduates, and non-educated women. The questionnaire for pupils, translated into English, is printed below. Upon the replies to this alone, the conclusions of this research are based.

QUESTIONNAIRE FOR PUPILS

Name of school:

Location (province, county, city):
Name of pupil:
Year and month of birth:

Age:

Place of birth:

How many months have you studied at this school?
What year of study is this? Please state clearly the year of lower primary, higher primary or middle school.
Do you live at home or at school?
Do you go home every week?
Do you expect to graduate or not?
How many years and months do you have yet in school before you graduate?
After you have finished school, what work do you expect to do?
Married or single?
Husband's occupation:
Father's occupation:
Father's yearly income:
Number of brothers and sisters:
Number of brothers and sisters in school:

42

What relatives have studied in China?
What relatives have studied abroad?
What intimate friends have studied in China?
What intimate friends have studied abroad?
Chart   I. Daily schedule of studies.
Chart   II. Schools previously attended.
          Names.
          Locations.
          Months in each.
Chart III. Subjects studied previously.
          Number of months' study in each.
          Number of recitations per week.
Chart IV. What did you do last Saturday?
          What did you do your last day at home?

Of 3000 pupil questionnaires sent out, 1176 answers, or 39.2 per cent, have been returned. The centers from which information was received are:

		Pupil Questionnaire	*Questionnaires Returned*	*Totals*
Chili Province	Changli	Alderman School	85	
(North China)	Peking	Gamewell School	2	
	Tientsin	Anglo-Chinese School	9	96
Fukien Province	Foochow	Foochow Girls' School	44	
		Hwa Nan School	35	
		Tao Hsu School	32	
		Yu Ying School	30	141
Kiangsi Province (Central China)	Kiukiang	Rulison School	98	98
Kiangsu Province	Shanghai	Bridgeman School	82	
		Chisiu School (Chinese Private)	21	
		McTyeire School	205	
		West Gate School (Chinese Private)	47	
	Nanking	Christian School	43	
		Gov't Higher Primary School	9	
		Gov't Normal School	15	
		Methodist School	67	489
Kwangtung Province (South China)	Canton	American Board School	31	
		Gov't Normal School	11	
		True Light Seminary	101	
		Union Normal School	12	155
Shantung Province (North China)	Hwai Yuan	Presbyterian School	48	48
Szechuan Province (West China)	Chengtu	Hwa Ying School	59	
		Union Normal School	16	
	Chungking	Shu Te School	36	
	Suining	Hwa Ying School	18	
	Tungchuanfu	Friend School	20	149
		Grand Total		1176

The answers to the pupil questionnaire have been received from every part of China, North, South, Central, West, and East. Twenty-six institutions are represented: 3 schools in Chili Province with 96 answers; 4 in Fukien Province with 141 answers; 1 in Kiangsi Province with 98 answers; 8 in Kiangsu Province with 489 answers; 4 in Kwangtung Province with 155 answers; 1 in Shantung Province with 48 answers; and 5 in Szechuan Province with 149 answers. Of the 26 institutions 21 are mission, 3 are government, and 2 are Chinese private schools. The last mentioned have been included although it is realized that general conclusions with regard to this group cannot be based on the returns from so small a number.[1]

All of the institutions from which adequate data were received are boarding schools. Day pupils from the immediate vicinity, however, usually attend. The majority of these institutions are higher primary and middle schools, with a preparatory lower primary department. Scholars who have attended or have graduated from other lower schools enter the higher primary and middle schools and thus the enrollment is increased. Hence it becomes apparent at the outset that we are studying a highly selected group, probably much superior to the group in the average lower primary schools.[2] The investigation does reveal, however, present tendencies in the elementary and secondary education of women in China.

---

[1] It is interesting to note, however, that brief comparisons of the individual government and private institutions with the general results found in this study do not show a wide variation.

[2] Cf. Part I, Chap. III, "Elimination in the School as a Whole."

CHAPTER II

THE SOCIAL ENVIRONMENT AND ASPIRATIONS OF THE CHINESE SCHOOLGIRL

SOCIAL STATUS

The traditional social divisions of Chinese society are: (1) Scholars, who include officials and the majority of the educated classes; (2) Farmers; (3) Artisans; (4) Merchants; and (5) Military Men and Servants. In the present changing order of society, these classes, which have never been separated by rigid lines, have become even less defined. Modern business pursuits and the professions are factors in society. The merchant and military groups have progressed more rapidly than the artisan and farmer classes. However, even to-day occupations fall naturally into these five classes, and with minor adaptations this grouping has been followed in this study. The professional men, and those who are engaged in work requiring higher education, are classified as scholars; the merchant class includes business men as well as those who are reported as merchants, and the fifth class mentioned above has been subdivided.

In view of these relatively important class divisions, it is desirable to learn whether or not the schoolgirl population, which is extremely small in number, comes from highly selected social groups. The report of the father's occupation was asked in each of the 1176 pupil questionnaires from the twenty-five schools. With the exception of a single institution in Shanghai, every school which sent answers to the questionnaire is represented in the returns. From the total number of 936 answers received, 2 which reported fathers in a foreign country but which did not state their occupation, 23 which reported fathers retired from active business, and 146 which reported fathers deceased are eliminated. Of the 765 remaining, 294, or 38.5 per cent, belong to the scholar class; 59, or 7.7 per cent, to the farmer; 11, or 1.4 per cent, to the artisan; 379, or 49.5 per cent, to the merchant; 21, or 2.7 per cent, to the servant, and 1, or 1 per cent, to the military classes.

FATHERS' OCCUPATIONS

	L.P.				H.P.			Middle				Prep.				H.S.				Prep. Nor.				Sp.	Total
	1	2	3	4	1	2	3	1	2	3	4	1	2	3	4	1	2	3	4	1	2	3	4		
Scholar Class:																									
Educators*	2	4		8	3	11	6	2	4	5	5		1					3	4	1	5	2	3	6	75
Engineers				2																					2
Lawyers	1		1		1																				3
Literary Men	1		1	3	4		1	1	1		3														14
Nurses					1																				1
Officials	3	1	1	4		7		6	6	1	2	1	2			6	4			1	2	4	1	9	57
Physicians	4	2	1	1	6	6	4		6	3	2		2		1	1	2			1	1			6	46
Religious Workers†	1		4	7	15	8	6	4	14	7	5	1	2					1	1	1	4		1	15	94
Students	1			1																					2
Total																									294
Farmer Class:																									
Farmers	1	1	3	9	3	3	1	1	3	2	2		1					4	1	1		1		23	59
Total																									59
Artisan Class:																									
Carpenters								1																	1
Printers																1	1			1				1	4
Skilled Workmen				1				1								1				1				1	5
Tanners	1																								1
Total																									11
Merchant Class:																									
General Business	7	14	11	28	15	22	3	16	10	7	9	1	6		5	2	6	8	1	1	3	8	3	21	185
Merchants	8	10	11	13	20	17	3	17	15	5	5	6	15		5	4	3	6	1			5		22	194
Total																									379
Military Class:																									
Military Men																					1				1
Total																									1
Servant Class:‡																									
Servants	2	3	1	2	1		3		1								1	1	2		1			3	21
Total																									21
Grand Total	28	36	25	80	69	75	26	46	57	28	31	9	21		11	10	20	33	10	6	11	19	7	107	765

* The Educators include teachers, and men engaged in direct educational work.
† The Religious Workers include Christian ministers and secretaries of the Young Men's Christian Association.
‡ The Servants include those engaged in unskilled labor, as well as servants.
L.P.—Lower Primary.   H.P.—Higher Primary.   Prep.—Preparatory.   H.S.—High School.   Prep. Nor.—Preparatory Normal.   Sp.—Special.

It is encouraging to note that the range of occupations included all grades of the social scale. Evidently no class as a class has failed to be reached by these schools. On the other hand, 88 per cent of the pupils come from the scholar and merchant classes. Nearly nine-tenths of the girls reporting belong to these groups, which probably comprise a relatively small proportion of the entire population of China.[1] This is especially significant in that it points to a probable selection of the fathers of the girls who attend school from the standpoint of general intelligence.

It has been customary in China for every family of the lower classes to set apart one of its members, usually the brightest one, for the scholar-representative, and all the others have worked to make him successful. This conscious selection through many generations may have produced a distinct superior-intelligence group. Probably the same selection, although less consciously brought about, has taken place among the business class. As the old traditional bonds of duty to the father's occupation have been broken, the keenly intellectual men have probably taken the lead and reconstructed business along progressive lines. The natural intellectual superiority of the average schoolgirl whose father has evidently more than ordinary ability is as yet unsupported by scientific investigation. But whether or not intellectual selection has taken place in the business and professional classes,[2] it is apparent from the data that the members of these groups are people of broad experience and progressive philosophies, who recognize the necessity of education for women.

The agricultural population of the nation is probably much larger than that of the professional class, and perhaps larger than that of the business class.[3] The daughters of the agricultural population are evidently little influenced by the schools, while those of the laboring and artisan classes are almost untouched. It seems likely that the fathers engaged in these occupations are often uneducated and traditional in their thinking. The need

---

[1] It is impossible to state accurate comparisons on account of the lack of census reports.

[2] The probability of such selection would seem to follow the conclusions of Terman. See Terman, L. M., *The Measurement of Intelligence*, p. 96.

[3] This statement is unsupported by census returns. However, it has been so estimated by students of China. See King, F. H., *Farmers of Forty Centuries*, p. 4.

and possibility for the education of their daughters has not been recognized by them. Further, social usages in the village community are often more rigid and more difficult to waive than in larger centers, and the daughter herself may hesitate to depart from popular custom. Again, there are few good schools in the country so that the country village girl must leave home if she would obtain even the most meagre education.[1]

The problem of the untouched classes is one of the greatest in Chinese education to-day. If the womanhood of China is to be educated, the girls whose fathers are farmers, laborers, and artisans must be reached. They have evidently been neglected and only conscious effort and propaganda directed to these classes by educators will make schooling possible for them.

ECONOMIC STATUS

The request for the report of the fathers' salaries was answered by very few of the pupils. Two hundred and twenty out of the 1176 reported both occupation and salary of their fathers. Nevertheless, from these few, some indications of the economic situation of the students may be found. The range of salary income is very great; from below \$100 Mexican[2] per year to \$50,000. However, the median salary falls just above \$500. The median salary of three educators is just above \$400; of five religious workers, \$100-\$199; of twenty-six officials, \$1000; of thirty-five business men, about \$500; of forty-six merchants, \$1000-\$1499. The median income of the three farmers reported is \$100; that of the printer and the ten servants, \$100.

The religious workers and the farmers seem to receive about equal salaries, but it may be that in the mission schools (where most of the daughters of religious workers attend) pastors' daughters receive certain perquisites. The meagre data at hand seem to indicate that economic and social cleavages follow approximately the same division lines. If the indications of the data may be taken as suggestive of a more widespread condition,[3]

---

[1] Cf. Part II, Chap. III.

[2] The Mexican dollar is worth about 50 cents gold in normal money markets. This standard is used uniformly throughout this study.

[3] This seems probable from the observation of students of China. Cf. Ross, E. A., *The Changing Chinese*, pp. 103-5, p. 338; Bashford, J. W., *China, An Interpretation*, pp. 49-52.

the question of providing adequate free educational facilities in communities where the economic status permits only the barest necessities of life, with probably insufficient food and clothing to supply the demands of health, is one that confronts the educator of Chinese girls to-day. Western standards of social necessities must be abandoned, and a new system of schoolgirl support worked out for China, whereby the girl of the poorer classes will be enabled to study, and at the same time not be too heavy a burden to her family. Probably the economic standards of life will be raised rapidly in the next decade. But at the present time, and during the period of change, careful experimentation

DETAILED TABULATION OF OCCUPATIONS OF FATHERS WITH SALARIES BELOW $1000

	Under $99	$100 to 199	200 to 299	300	400	500	600	700	800	900	Total
Scholar Class:											
Educators	2	8	4	1	2	3	1	1	1	1	24
Nurses											
Officials		1	3		1	1			3	4	13
Physicians							1	1			2
Religious Workers	13	19	8	4	3			1		2	50
The Artisan Class:											
Printers		2									2
Tanners	1										1
The Farmer Class:											
Farmers	1	1	1								3
The Merchant Class:											
General Business	5	4	3		1	2			2		17
Merchants	3	1	1	1	2	3		1	1	1	14
The Servant Class:											
Servants	5	1	4								10
Grand Total	30	37	24	6	9	9	2	4	7	8	136

and thoughtful effort will be needed to extend to the girl of the lower economic classes the privilege of an education to which she has a right. The problem of self support for these girls who ought to be in school while conditions are changing, is one of the outstanding problems for educational administrators.

HOME RELATIONSHIPS

Usually the girls' schools above the lower primary school are boarding schools. In order to learn the extent to which the girls are separated from life in the home, the questions "Do you live at home or at school?" and "Do you go home every week?"

were asked, and 1084 answers were received.   Of the girls who replied, 183, or 16.8 per cent, live at home; 21, or 1.9 per cent, live with relatives; and 880, or 81.1 per cent, live in the dormitories.

OCCUPATIONS AND

	$499	500 to 999	1000 to 1499	1500 to 1999	2000 to 2499	2500 to 2999	3000 to 3499	3500 to 3999	4000 to 4499	4500 to 4999	5000 to 5499
Scholar Class:											
Educators	17	7	3	3			2				
Engineers											
Lawyers											
Literary Men											
Nurses											
Officials	5	8			3		4			1	
Physicians		2	4						2		
Religious Workers	47	3	1								
Students											
Farmer Class:											
Farmers	3										
Artisan Class:											
Carpenters											
Printers	2										
Skilled Workmen											
Tanners	1										
Merchant Class:											
General Business Men	13	4	8	2	2			5			1
Merchants	8	6	10	2	2		3		4		1
Military Class:											
Military Men			1								
Servant Class:											
Servants	10										
Totals	106	30	27	7	7		9	5	6	1	2

Of those living at the school, 163, or 15 per cent, go home every week; 98, or 9 per cent, go home every month; 19, or 1.7 per cent, go home sometimes, and 595, or 54.9 per cent, do not go home.[1]   We may thus infer that more than half of the schoolgirls are away from their homes for the entire school year, except perhaps for brief between-semester visits. It will be seen from the following tables that the majority of the girls live at home for the first and second years in the lower primary school.   But from the third year lower primary until they leave school the greater number live in school dormitories.

The separation of more than one half of the schoolgirls of China from their homes during the period of education is of grave import.   At best the girls will acquire habits of thought and

---

[1] Five left the answers to visits home blank.

action different from those people in the home who have little or no education,[1] and unless the contacts are sufficiently close to keep a common sympathy, there must be a strong tendency for

SALARIES OF FATHERS

5500 to 5999	6000 to 6499	6500 to 6900	7000 to 7499	7500 to 7999	8000 to 8499	8500 to 8999	9000 to 9499	9500 to 9999	10000	19000	20000	30000	50000	Total
									1			1		33
														1
									1					1
					2				2				1	26
			2											10
														51
														3
														2
														1
	5				1				2	1	1			35
														46
														1
														10
	5		2		3				6	1	1	1	1	220

the girls to become isolated from their homes and communities. The traditional idea of education separated from life, and the externally imposed Western education serve to accentuate the tendency.   It is very possible that one reason why the daughters of the lower social and economic classes are not sent to school is because the families fear estrangement.   Thus, if education is to be a growth for the girls in school, and at the same time to be an integral service to society, educators will need to guard against desocializaion of the girls while in school, and to direct their attention to the strengthening of the bonds between the school and home community life.[2]

---

[1] The large proportion of women in the homes to-day, even among professional and business classes, are uneducated.   Education thus tends to separate girls from their mothers.

[2] See discussion under Curriculum.

RESIDENCE AND GRADE

	L. P.				H. P.			Middle				Prep.				H. S.				N. P.	Nor.				Sp.	Total
	1	2	3	4	1	2	3	1	2	3	4	1	2	3	4	1	2	3	4		1	2	3	4		
Members Living at Home	31	37	12	29	3	4		6	5	1		7	12				4	3	1			1	8	2		18	184
With Relatives	1	2			1	2	1	2	2							1	1						4	3		2	20
In Dormitories	3	7	17	94	78	97	39	65	86	36	55	4	11	11	5	14	22	41	15	6	16	17	6		135	880
Totals	35	46	29	123	82	103	40	73	93	37	55	11	23	11	5	15	27	44	16	6	17	29	11		153	1084

HOME VISITS AND GRADE

	L. P.				H. P.			Middle				Prep.				H. S.				N. P.	Nor.				Sp.	Total
	1	2	3	4	1	2	3	1	2	3	4	1	2	3	4	1	2	3	4		1	2	3	4		
Visits at Home: Once a week	1	6	3	16	3	13	2	29	15	3	11	3	7	8	5	10	2	3	2	2	3	1			15	163
Once a month				3	30	20	10	3	8	5	12						1	1				3			2	98
Sometimes					2	1	3	2	2	3	1						1	3					1			19
Do Not Visit Home	2	1	14	73	43	62	24	31	60	25	31	1	4	3		4	18	34	13	4	13	13	4		118	595
Totals	3	7	17	92	78	96	39	65	85	36	55	4	11	11	5	14	22	41	15	6	16	17	5		135	875

L. P.—Lower Primary.   H. P.—Higher Primary.   Prep.—Preparatory.   H. S.—High School.   Prep. Nor.—Preparatory Normal.   Sp.—Special.

AMBITIONS

Subject	L.P. 1	L.P. 2	L.P. 3	H.P. 1	H.P. 2	H.P. 3	H.P. 4	Middle 1	Middle 2	Middle 3	Middle 4	Prep. 1	Prep. 2	Prep. 3	Prep. 4	N.P.	H.S. 1	H.S. 2	H.S. 3	H.S. 4	Normal 1	Normal 2	Normal 3	Normal 4	Sp.	Total
Business		1		1	1																1				1	5
Evangelism				4	10	7	2		6	1	1							2	4						1	40
Fine Arts												1														1
Further Study	9	8	7	28	31	42	11	10	14	4	14	1					3	4	14	1		4			22	227
Handwork								1																		1
Rendering Help to Brothers								1	1	1	1															4
Home-keeping									1																	1
Kindergartening										1	1									1	1					4
Medicine	1	3		7	6	7	4	6	6	1	4		9				1	3	3						5	66
Music				2	2	2	1												1							8
Nursing				2	2	1																			1	6
Physical Education																			1							1
Social Work														2					1							3
Travel																								2		2
Travel in Foreign County	1	1						1					13													16
Teaching	13	12	10	40	21	15	7	24	34	17	19	8	1	6	5		3	9	6	1	2	7	20	4	26	303
Not specified	7	16	5	23	11	26	15	24	15	6	11						5	7	8	11	2		6	2	78	296
Study in Foreign Country		2						2	1																1	8
Total	31	43	22	107	83	101	42	69	82	36	52	10	23	10	5		13	25	38	14	6	11	26	8	135	992

AMBITIONS

In order to learn what place the girl herself desired to fill in society, the question "After you have finished school, what work do you expect to do?" was asked. That this group of schoolgirls is selected by ambition for intellectual pursuits seems very evident from the 992 direct replies received to this question. In fact, their ambition for study doubtless has been a large factor in their entrance to and continuation in school. Six hundred and sixty-one out of the total number expect to become students in higher institutions; teachers, evangelists, physicians, musicians, social workers, business women, and nurses. The four ranking highest in popularity are distributed as follows: 303 desire to teach, 227 hope for further study, 66 plan to study medicine, 40 plan to become evangelists, and 296 are uncertain. Only one states that she desires home life. About one half show no definite recognition of social relationship in their ambition (i.e., "students" and "uncertain"), the other half state purposes of distinct service to society, i.e., those who intend to enter the work of teaching, medicine, evangelism, and social work.

The limited number of occupations chosen by the girls is probably due to the fact that very few occupations are as yet open to women. The stated purpose, however, of so large a number who plan to become teachers is relatively significant. With the rapid increase in the number of schools, which will doubtless take place within the next decade, there will be a great need for trained teachers. Probably many of the girls who hope to continue study, expect to teach when graduated. The choice of five of the girls for business, and of three of the girls for social work, shows that these fields will probably be developed for women in the near future. Although only one girl definitely stated her desire for home life, doubtless the majority of the girls will eventually enter homes of their own.

It is apparent that although these schoolgirls have expressed their ambitions to enter these vocations, this fact cannot be taken as proof that they will do so. Nevertheless, the report does show the general lines along which they will desire training. The schools will need to recognize these factors in shaping their curricula to meet social needs. To select each study so that it may contribute both to the needs of society and to the desires of the individual, is an immediate need of education in China today.

CHAPTER III

THE CLASSIFICATION OF PUPILS

AGE-DISTRIBUTION

The comparison of age with grade has been a very difficult undertaking. Although the question was specific in Chinese, literally, "What year of study is this? (state clearly the year of the lower primary, higher primary, or middle school)" the answers varied greatly. Unfortunately, many of the mission schools do not follow the general nomenclature of the government, and thus "high school"[1] might mean higher primary or (following the American nomenclature, literally translated) middle school. It may be that in some cases "middle school" is used as a term for higher primary school, although this does not seem likely. In one institution, "preparatory school," probably a term for middle school is reported. It may be, also, that some of the girls do not know in which grade to consider themselves. In every case, however, the translation has been as exact as possible, and every girl whose grade was doubtful is classed "special."

The questions regarding age and grade were answered in a more or less accurate way by all of the 1176 pupils; of these, however, 6 failed to give their ages, and 216 were unable to give their grades clearly. Of the 1176, 239 are in the lower primary school, 234 in the higher primary school, 267 in the middle school,[2] 54 in the preparatory school, 103 in the high school, and 63 in the normal school. The table on page 56 shows the age-grade distribution in the twenty-six schools of the study.

The legal school entrance age of a Chinese child is 6; thus the youngest of the 1170 girls reporting ages in the questionnaires is 6 years old. The oldest is 34. Only six of the 115 girls in the first grade lower primary are 6 years old; only three are 7 years old.

---

[1] In the third year of high school the age range was from 10 to 20 years in but 44 cases. The only possible explanation seems to be a misunderstanding as to the meaning of the question.

[2] The reason for the large number of pupils in the higher grades is that boarding-schools tend to become institutions to which graduates of smaller schools come for more advanced study.

AGE AND GRADE

Age	6	7	8	9	10	11	12	13	14	15	16	17	18	19	20	21	22	23	24	25	26	27	28	29	34	Bl.*	Total
1 Lower Primary	6	3		6	1	3	3	7	1	1	1	2	1														37
2 Lower Primary		1	5	6	5	13	6	8	2	2	1	3															47
3 Lower Primary				1	3	3	5	9	15	20	22	2															31
4 Lower Primary					1	5	9	30	12	18	11	8	7	2	1												124
1 Higher Primary						2	6	6	13	20	23	14	10	3	3												86
2 Higher Primary						1	4	6	6	4	5	14	17	7	2	1											106
3 Higher Primary							1	1	5	9	12	7	10	4	1	1											42
1 Middle						1		1		4	13	16	17	12	10	7	2										74
2 Middle								1		2	2	15	22	21	8	1	1										97
3 Middle											1	8	4	6	12	9	10	1									38
4 Middle					1								6	14	2	1									1		58
1 Preparatory							3	3	2	2	2	1	1	1	1	1											14
2 Preparatory							1	1	4	6	3	4	1	4	1			1									23
3 Preparatory								2	2	9	2	4	9		1			1									11
4 Preparatory										2	3	1	4	4	1			1	1								6
1 High School							1	3	2	2	3	1	2	7	2			1									16
2 High School							1	1	2	3	6	5	1	1	1	1		1	1								27
3 High School								2	2		8	5	9	4	3	1		1	1		1					1	44
4 High School										1	2	7	4	4	7	3	1	2		1							16
Prep. Normal											1	2	2	1	2					2							6
1 Normal School												3	4	4	1	1	1	1	1	1	1		1			1	17
2 Normal School											5	5	4	4	2	3	1	1		2						2	29
3 Normal School											2	1	6	1		3		2									11
Special (grade uncertain)			1							1																	216
Total	**6**	**6**	**7**	**1**	**13**	**34**	**44**	**89**	**86**	**142**	**161**	**162**	**150**	**120**	**65**	**27**	**19**	**11**	**4**	**5**	**2**	**1**	**1**	**1**	**1**	**6**	**1176**

* Not reporting.

The median age of the girls in the first year of school is 9.83 years ± .434 P.E. (4.5 P.E. − 1.953).

The median entrance age of the girls in the second year of school is 11.92 years ± .323 (4.5 P.E. − 1.453). In the third year lower primary, the median age is 13.44 years ± .376 P.E. (4.5 P.E. − 1.692). Thus the median age of the girls in their first year of school is 9.83 years, or almost four years above the legal entrance age. After one year of school work, the median age is 11.92 years, almost six years above the legal entrance age, and fully two years above the median age of the first year. The median age of the third year of school is 13.44 years, nearly seven and one-half years above the legal entrance age, and fully one and one-half years above the median age of the second year. The median age of the fourth lower primary is 15.3 years ± .18 P.E. (4.5 P.E. − .824), over nine years above the legal entrance age, and over one and one-half years above the median age of the third year.

In the higher primary school, the median age of the girls in the first grade is 15.92 years ± .594 P.E. (4.5 P.E. − 2.671); of those in the second, 16.31 years ± .169 (4.5 P.E. − 1.37); and of those in the third, 18. 64 years ± .304 (4.5 P.E. − 1.37).

The median ages of the middle school are: 17.49 years ± .17 P.E. (4.5 P.E. − .81); 18.73 years ± .3 P.E. (4.5 P.E. − 1.35); 18.88 years ± .344 P.E. (4.5 P.E. − 1.55); and 20.54 years ± .224 (4.5 P.E. − .1). Those of the preparatory school are: 15.42 ± .398 (4.5 P.E. − 1.79), 15.78 ± .458 (4.5 P.E. − 2.06), 17 ± .475 (4.5 P.E. − 2.14), and 16.5 ± .378 (4.5 P.E. − 1.71) for each successive year.

The median ages of the high school are: 16.17 ± .513 P.E. (4.5 P.E. − 2.31), 17.2 ± .415 (4.5 P.E. − 1.86), 17.1 ± .27 (4.5 P.E. − 1.21), 17.79 ± .328 (4.5 P.E. − 1.48). The median age of the preparatory normal group is 18.25 ± .42 (4.5 P.E. − 1.89); of the first year normal, 19 ± .985 (4.5 P.E. − 4.43); of the second year normal, 20.4 ± .41 P.E. (4.5 P.E. − 1.83); of the third year normal, 19 ± .53 (4.5 P.E. − 2.43); of the special group, 17.19 ± .169 (4.5 P.E. − .76).

The median age of the total group is 16.39 years ± .08 (4.5 P.E. −.36).

The 25 percentile is at 14.9 years and the 75 percentile at 18.8 years. That is, 50 per cent of the pupils are between 14.9 years and 18.8 years old.   The table shows that dropping out of schools does not appear to be a serious factor until the age of eighteen. Thus it seems probable that the actual school period of the Chinese boarding-school girl is from about ten until nineteen years of age.

The data show conclusively that the entrance age of the majority of Chinese girls is from three to seven years higher than the legal entrance age.   This is probably due to the traditional hesitancy in allowing girls to study.   It is also probably due to the fact that girls who are away from the centers have no schools near and so must attend boarding schools, and parents dislike to send the girls away from home too young.   Although the Chinese girl learns much from life in the home, and obtains a close sympathy with the traditions of family life, yet four, and often more, of the most valuable educational years are allowed to pass, and the tools of education, reading and writing, are not mastered until comparatively late.

The fact that the median age is more than one year later in each successive grade in the lower primary school may be explained in three ways.   It is possible that because of the rapid increase of the popularity of girls' schools during the last few years, the median school entrance age of each year has been earlier. Again, older girls, entering the second, third, and fourth grades from outside institutions may materially add to the median age of these years.   Or, it may be that progress is slow, and that for many pupils time is lost through non-promotion.   A study of one group from year to year would reveal the rate of progress.   Accurate school promotion records will give the data required. Such a study is necessary before the actual waste of time in school may be ascertained.

The data also show that these girls do not leave school at fourteen years of age, but remain for eight or nine consecutive years.   There are several reasons why these girls are permitted to continue their study uninterrupted.   In the first place, the schoolgirls of the higher primary and middle schools are a selected group, from the homes of the educated classes.   Their families expect them to remain in school.   Again, the number of girls in China who are in school, when compared with the total population of girls of school age, is very small, and those in school appreciate the privilege of learning to read.   They therefore apply themselves earnestly to study. In addition to this, the industrial and commercial worlds are not yet open to women, and do not offer an immediate opportunity for self-support. The limited number of callings open to women necessitates preparation in school. At the same time, government and mission scholarships make it possible for the schoolgirl to remain at school with a minimum cost to her parents. Moreover, the educated girl does not marry before she is 17 or 18 years of age. As a result, she

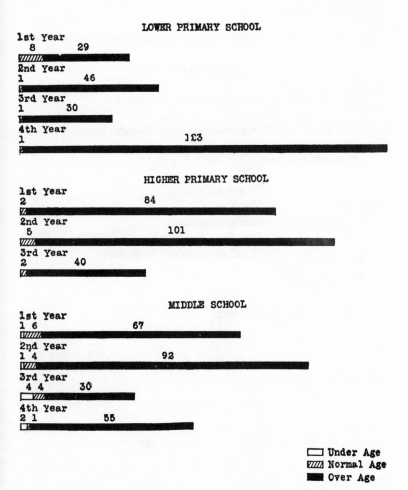

FIG. 5. AGE-GRADE DISTRIBUTION (BASED ON LEGAL ENTRANCE AGE).

may have the years from the time she is old enough to leave home, until her marriage, free to engage in study.

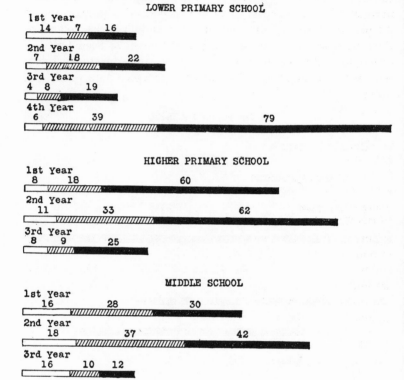

FIG. 6. AGE-GRADE DISTRIBUTION (BASED ON MEDIUM ENTRANCE AGE).

AMOUNT OF UNDER-AGE,[1] NORMAL-AGE[2] AND OVER-AGE[3]

From the late school entrance age, and the slow rate of progress, it follows that the amount of over-age present is extremely

---

[1] "Under-age" is a term applied to the age of pupils in any grade of the school system who are younger than they would be had they entered at legal age and progressed one grade each year.

(Notes [2] and [3] on page 61.)

great. In the first grade lower primary, in spite of late entrance, the proportion of over-age is less than in any other grade; taking the legal entrance age as a basis, 24.3 per cent of the pupils are of normal age and 75.6 per cent are over-age. In the second grade, 2.1 per cent are normal and 97.8 per cent are over-age. In the third grade, 3.2 per cent are of normal age and 96.7 per cent are over-age. In the fourth grade, .8 per cent are normal and 99.1 per cent are over-age. The same conditions hold for the higher primary school, although in the last two years the percentage of over-age is slightly less. In the first year of the higher primary, 2.3 per cent are normal age and 97.6 per cent over-age; in the second year of the higher primary, 4.7 per cent are of normal age and 95.2 per cent are over-age. In the third year of the higher primary, 4.7 per cent are normal age and 95.2 per cent are over-age. The first under-age is shown in the first year of the middle school, and is present to some extent in each of the four years. In the first year of the middle school, 1.3 per cent are under-age, 8.1 per cent are normal, and 90.5 per cent are over-age. In the second year, 1.0 per cent are under-age, 4.1 per cent are normal, and 94.8 per cent are over-age. In the third year, 10.5 per cent are under-age, 10.5 per cent normal, and 78.9 per cent are over-age. In the fourth year, 3.4 per cent are under-age, 1.7 per cent are normal, and 94.8 per cent over-age.

---

[2] "Normal-age" is a term applied to the age of pupils in any grade of the school system who are in the grade and of the age they would be had they entered at legal age. It is customary, however, to consider both six and seven as ages of normal entrance. Cf. Strayer, G. D., *Some Problems in City Administration*, pp. 70, 76, 77.

[3] "Over-age" is a term applied to the age of pupils in any grade of the school system who are older than they would be had they entered at legal age, and progressed one grade each year.

TABLE OF AGE-GRADE DISTRIBUTIONS* SHOWING DEGREE OF OVER-AGE WITH LEGAL ENTRANCE AGE AS STANDARD

Age	6	7	8	9	10	11	12	13	14	15	16	17	18	19	20	21	22	23	24	25	26	27	28	29	Bl.	Total
1 Lower Primary	6	3	5	6	1	3	3	7																		37
2 Lower Primary		1		6	5	13	6	8	1	1	1	3														47
3 Lower Primary				1	3	3	5	9	2	2	2	2	1	2												31
4 Lower Primary					1	5	9	30	15	20	22	8	7	3	1					1						124
1 Higher Primary						2	6	6	12	18	11	14	10	7												86
2 Higher Primary							4	6	12	20	24	14	17	4	3		1	1						1		106
3 Higher Primary						1	1	1	6	4	5	7	10	4	2	1	1	1								42
1 Middle								1	5	9	12	16	17	12		2										74
2 Middle								1	4	5	13	15	22	21	10	5	1	1							1	97
3 Middle										2	4	8	4	6	8	1	1	1	1	1	1					38
4 Middle										1	1	2	6	14	12	9	10	1	1	1					1	58
Total	6	4	5	13	10	28	34	69	57	82	94	89	94	73	37	20	13	5	1	2	1			1	2	740

* Numbers within the heavy lines show the number of pupils in each grade who are of normal age: numbers at the left show under-age, and at the right, over-age.

PERCENTAGE OF UNDER-AGE, NORMAL-AGE AND OVER-AGE PUPILS ON
THE BASIS OF LEGAL ENTRANCE AGE

	Under-Age	Normal-Age	Over-Age
1 Lower Primary		24.3%	75.6%
2 Lower Primary		2.1%	97.8%
3 Lower Primary		3.2%	96.7%
4 Lower Primary		.8%	99.1%
1 Higher Primary		2.3%	97.6%
2 Higher Primary		4.7%	95.2%
3 Higher Primary		4.7%	95.2%
1 Middle School	1.3%	8.1%	90.5%
2 Middle School	1.0%	4.1%	94.8%
3 Middle School	10.5%	10.5%	78.9%
4 Middle School	3.4%	1.7%	94.8%
Total	1.0%	4.7%	94.1%

If, instead of on the basis of the legal age of school entrance,
the median entrance age, with the age just one year older, is
taken as a basis, the amount of over-age is as shown on page 64.

PERCENTAGE OF UNDER-AGE, NORMAL-AGE AND OVER-AGE PUPILS ON
THE BASIS OF MEDIAN ENTRANCE AGE

	Under-Age	Normal-Age	Over-Age
1 Lower Primary	37.8%	18.9%	48.2%
2 Lower Primary	14.9%	38.2%	46.8%
3 Lower Primary	12.9%	25.8%	61.2%
4 Lower Primary	4.8%	31.4%	63.7%
1 Higher Primary	9.3%	20.9%	69.7%
2 Higher Primary	10.3%	31.1%	58.4%
3 Higher Primary	9.7%	21.4%	59.5%
1 Middle School	21.6%	37.8%	41.6%
2 Middle School	18.5%	38.1%	43.2%
3 Middle School	42.1%	26.3%	31.5%
4 Middle School	15.7%	45.6%	38.6%
Total	15.6%	31.4%	52.7%

Here again over-age is present to a marked degree. In the
first year lower primary, 14, or 37.8 per cent, are under-age, only
7, or 18.9 per cent, are of normal age, and 16, or 43.2 per cent,
are over-age. For the next four years, the degree of over-age
grows steadily larger: 7, or 14.9 per cent, in the second year
lower primary are under-age, 18, or 38.2 per cent, normal age,
and 46.8 per cent over-age; in the third year lower primary, 4, or
12.9 per cent, are under-age, 8, or 25.8 per cent, normal age, and
61.2 per cent over-age; in the fourth year lower primary, 6, or 4.8
per cent, are under-age, 39, or 31.4 per cent, normal age, and 79,
or 63.7 per cent, over-age; in the first year higher primary, 8, or

TABLE OF AGE-GRADE DISTRIBUTIONS* SHOWING DEGREE OF OVER-AGE WITH MEDIAN ENTRANCE AGE AS STANDARD

Age	6	7	8	9	10	11	12	13	14	15	16	17	18	19	20	21	22	23	24	25	26	27	28	29	Bl.	Total
1 Lower Primary	6	3	5	6	1	3	3	7			1	2														37
2 Lower Primary		1		6	5	13	6	8			1	3														47
3 Lower Primary				1	3	3	5	9	1	1	2	2	1													31
4 Lower Primary					1	5	9	30	15	20	22	8	6	3												124
1 Higher Primary							2	6	12	18	11	14	7	7	1			2								86
2 Higher Primary							4	6	13	20	23	14	10	4	2	1										106
3 Higher Primary							1	1	6	4	5	7	10	4	1	1								1		42
1 Middle						1		1	5	9	12	16	13	12	3	1			1							74
2 Middle										4	13	15	21	21	10	7	2	1	1	1					1	97
3 Middle												8	11	6	8	1	1	1	1		1					38
4 Middle													9	14	12	9	10	1	1	1					1	58
Total	6	4	5	13	10	28	34	69	58	82	93	89	94	73	37	20	13	5	5	2	1			1	2	740

* Numbers within the heavy lines show the number of pupils in each grade who are of normal age, numbers at the left show under-age, and at the right, over-age.

9.3 per cent, are under-age, 18, or 20.9 per cent, normal age, and 60, or 69.7 per cent, over-age. In the second year higher primary, the fact that the eighteen or nineteen-year-old girls are leaving school affects the proportion of over-age. Here 11, or 10.3 per cent, are under-age, 33, or 31.1 per cent, normal, and 62, or 58.4 per cent, over-age. In third year higher primary, 9.7 per cent are under-age, 21.4 per cent normal, and 25, or 59.5 per cent, over-age. In the middle school in the first year, 16, or 21.6 per cent, are under-age, 28, or 37.8 per cent, normal, and 41.6 per cent over-age; in the second year, 18, or 18.5 per cent, are under-age, 37, or 38.1 per cent, normal, and 42, or 43.2 per cent, over-age; in the third year, 16, or 42.1 per cent, are under-age, 10, or 26.3 per cent, normal, and 12, or 31.5 per cent, over-age; in the fourth year, 9, or 15.7 per cent, are under-age, 26, or 45.6 per cent, normal, and 22, or 38.6 per cent, over-age. In the middle school, the effect of the leaving age is naturally very marked, since the normal age on the basis of the median age of the first middle grade is 18 or 19 years of age.

Thus it is evident that even upon the basis of the four years late median age of the first year of school, the succeeding years of school contain a large number of over-age pupils. It may be concluded, therefore, that the schools at the present time are dealing with a group of older girls in the lower school grades, and that these girls will have only eight or nine consecutive years in school. To enable the pupils to make the best possible use of this limited time, each should be given tasks that challenge her best effort. Older pupils who will spend only one or two years in school, and who have learned to cook and sew at home will need a very different course from young pupils in the same grade, who have never learned the essentials of home-keeping, and who will probably remain at school for ten or twelve years. Individual freedom in the choice of courses, especially on the part of those who are older, is important in all grades. Younger pupils who have proved their ability should be encouraged to progress rapidly through the system, and thus secure ample time for preparation for the professions. When it is found that a large proportion of the pupils take longer than the scheduled time to complete certain courses, adjustment of the courses to the ability of the girls should be made. This will necessitate flexible grade divisions with frequent promotion, special rooms for over-age and under-age pupils and a wide variation of subjects.[1]   Adequate solutions to the various phases of this problem can be worked out only by conscious experiment and comparison of results in China.

---

[1] For efforts to meet similar situations in America, cf. Cubberley, E. P., *Public School Administration*, Chap. XVII–XVIII; Strayer, G. D., *Some Problems in City School Administration*, Chap. VI, VIII, XII.

CHAPTER IV

THE SUBJECTS IN THE CURRICULUM

The studies reported by the girls in the schools closely follow the courses outlined in the government and mission curricula. In the First Year Lower Primary, 34 of the 37 girls reported weekly schedules. The subjects reported by the highest number of girls are: Chinese reading, by 32 of the 34 girls of that grade reporting; arithmetic, 30; singing, 27; English and Bible, each 26; geography and writing, each 23. English grammar is reported by 4 of the girls. In addition to the 26 reporting Bible, 18 report moral training as a part of their weekly schedules; 18 also report physical training. Of the newer subjects hand-work is reported by 3, and stories by 1.

The proportion of time spent on each subject is also given in the schedule. Whenever the periods given were irregular, or the time specified uncertain, the number of hours is listed under "Not Reporting." Thus the proportion of time is approximately accurate. Five hours per week is spent on arithmetic by 20 of the girls, on English by 22, on geography by 14, and on writing by 17. Bible is studied 3 hours a week by 14. Eleven girls spend 2 hours a week on physical training.

SUBJECTS OF STUDY—FIRST LOWER PRIMARY

Number of Recitation Periods per Week	1	2	3	4	5	6	7	8	9	10	Not Reporting	Total
Chinese Reading		2			19					1	10	32
Arithmetic	2		1		20						7	30
Singing		4	9	1	5						8	27
Bible		2	14		8						2	26
English	1				22						3	26
Geography	2	4			14						3	23
Writing	1		2		17						3	23
Moral Training		13	3		1						1	18
Physical Training		11	2		4						1	18
Composition	1	2	1	2	1						1	8
Grammar		1			3							4
Drawing	2	1										3
Hand-work											3	3
Botany					1						1	2
English Writing					2							2
History											1	1
Music	1											1
Stories											1	1

Number of girls in First Lower Primary, 37; number reporting schedules, 34.

In the Second Year Lower Primary the subjects are practically the same.   Singing is reported by 41 of the 45 girls; arithmetic by 39; Chinese reading by 39; geography by 37; writing by 37; Bible by 36; English by 35; drawing by 29; and physical training by 29.   Three report hand-work, 2 report manual arts, and 2 report stories.   The proportion of time is given as follows: 16 spend 3 hours on arithmetic; 25 spend 5 hours on Bible; 14 spend 3 hours, and 8 spend 5 hours on Chinese reading.   Sixteen spend 2 hours on drawing; 26 spend 5 hours on English; 18 spend 2 hours on geography; 14, 2 hours on grammar; 14, 2 hours on moral training; 19, 2 hours on physical training; 28, 2 hours on singing; and 28, 5 hours on writing.

SUBJECTS OF STUDY—SECOND LOWER PRIMARY

Number of Recitation Periods Per Week	1	2	3	4	5	6	7	8	12	13	17	Not Reporting	Total
Singing	2	28	1		1	3						6	41
Arithmetic	1	2	16	2	10	2						6	39
Chinese Reading	1	14	3	1	8	1		1			1	9	39
Geography		18	3		8	1						7	37
Writing	1	2			28	1						5	37
Bible		2	2		25	1						6	36
English		1	1		26	1		1	1	1		3	35
Drawing	8	16	1		2							2	29
Physical Training	1	19	6		1	1						1	29
Moral Training	2	14				1						2	19
Grammar	1	14			1							1	17
Composition	2	3	1									1	7
Botany	1	1			1	1						2	6
Hand-work			1		1							1	3
Manual Arts	1											1	2
Stories			1									1	2
History	1												1
Letter Writing	1												1
Music		1											1

Number of girls in Second Lower Primary, 47; number reporting sechedules, 45.

In the Third Year Lower Primary arithmetic, reported by 28 of the 31 girls; Chinese reading, reported by 30; Bible, reported by 29; geography, reported by 25; physical training, reported by 21; and writing, reported by 24, lead the subjects.   Only 13 of the 31 girls report English in this grade.   Hand-work and manual training are reported by 4, sanitation by 6, and sewing by 5.   The proportion of time on each of these studies is given by only a scattering few.

The studies of the Fourth Year Lower Primary were reported by 118 out of the total of 124 girls: 111 are studying Chinese reading; 107, arithmetic; 103, geography; 98, Bible; 75, writing;

SUBJECTS OF STUDY—THIRD LOWER PRIMARY

Number of Recitation Periods Per Week	1	2	3	4	5	6	7	8	9	12	Not Reporting	Total
Chinese Reading	1				8	2	1		3		15	30
Bible		6	2	1	4	2				1	13	29
Arithmetic		1			8	3	3				13	28
Geography	5	4	4		2						10	25
Writing	2	2			5	1	1				13	24
Physical Training	2	4	1		6						8	21
English			1		2						10	13
Moral Training	2	3			1						5	11
Singing	3	2	1		1						4	11
Drawing	2	6									1	9
History		6			1						2	9
Sanitation	5		1									6
Sewing	1	4										5
Ethics	4											4
Manual Training	3											3
Art	2											2
Classics								1			1	2
Music			1		1							2
Natural Science	1						1					2
Composition				1								1
English Writing			1									1
Hand-work	1											1
Mental Arithmetic					1							1
Piano		1										1

Number of girls in Third Lower Primary, 31; number reporting schedules, 31.

SUBJECTS OF STUDY—FOURTH LOWER PRIMARY

Number of Recitation Periods Per Week	1	2	3	4	5	6	7	8	9	10	Not Reporting	Total
Chinese Reading	4	6	5	3	32	1	5	3	8	3	41	111
Arithmetic	4	5	3	3	52	1	8			1	30	107
Geography	12	29	4	3	18						37	103
Bible	4	28	14	1	16	1				1	33	98
Writing	10	10	6	3	23						23	75
English		3	2	3	26					4	34	72
History	3	24	12	1	3						22	65
Drawing	21	23			2						12	58
Physical Education	5	18	3		14						18	58
Singing	14	10	7	1	4						21	57
Grammar	4	3	2	2	8						15	34
Composition	12	18	1	1								32
Moral Training	2	5	2		1						13	23
Sewing	3	13			1						6	23
General Science	7	2	3		1	1					7	21
Ethics	11	1	2		2						3	19
Classics	1	3	2	1	2					1	6	16
Sanitation	9	2	2								3	16
Essay	7	1			1						6	15
Letter Writing	14	1										15
Hand-work	6	3			2						2	13
Music		2	1		3						6	12
Physics			3		7						1	11
Hygiene		5									5	10
Art	3				5							8
Recitations		1	7									8
Chemistry											5	5
Foreign History	1	2									1	4
Piano					1						1	2
Domestic Science	1											1
Manual Training	1											1
Mental Arithmetic					1							1

Number of girls in First Higher Primary, 124; number reporting schedules, 118.

72, English; 65, history; 58, physical education; 58, drawing; and 57, singing; 23, sewing; 16, sanitation; 13, hand-work; 1, manual training; and 1, domestic science.

Although the period schedule varies from 1 to 5 periods in most of the subjects, and for arithmetic, Chinese, and English from 1 to 10 periods, usually arithmetic, Chinese reading, English and writing are accorded 5 recitation periods per week; Bible, drawing, geography, history, physical training, and sewing, 2 periods; and sanitation, domestic science and hand-work, 1 period per week. Twenty-three give drawing 2 periods per week; 21, 1 period per week.

In the First Year Higher Primary, the total number, 86, reported weekly schedules of recitation periods: 73 are studying arithmetic; 73, Chinese reading; 72, geography; 69, Bible; 68,

SUBJECTS OF STUDY—FIRST HIGHER PRIMARY

Number of Recitation Periods Per Week	1	2	3	4	5	6	7	8	9	10	12	Not Reporting	Total
Arithmetic		31	1		23							18	73
Chinese Reading		6		8	40	1		1	1			16	73
Geography		1	38	1	3							29	72
Bible	1	6	30	2	6							24	69
History		32	8		7							21	68
English		1	1	1	42			3		2	1	12	63
Physical Training		33	1	1	2							14	51
Singing	29	2	4		1							12	48
Drawing	25	8										7	40
Writing	2	2	1		14							18	37
Composition	31	2	1									1	35
Sewing	29											5	34
Letter Writing	2	29										1	32
Music	7	13	2									4	26
Essay	16	3	1		1							6	27
General Science		1	3	4	2							15	25
Hand-work	13		1	1	1							2	18
Art	1		2	1	11							2	17
Moral Training		3			5							8	16
Classics		3	1		4							2	10
Sanitation					6							2	8
Ethics		1										6	7
Physiology		3	1	1	1							1	7
Mencius					1							5	6
Mandarin		1										3	4
Religion		1			1							1	3
Five Books					1					1			2
Rhetoric		1										1	2
Map Drawing												2	2
Agriculture	1												1
Physics		1											1

Number of girls in Second Higher Primary, 86; number reporting schedules, 86.

history; and 63, English; 34, sewing; 18, hand-work; 8, sanitation; and 4, Mandarin.[1] Thirty-one spend 2 recitation hours per

[1] The language which is most universally spoken in China, and which will probably become the national language.

week on arithmetic, and 23, 5 recitation hours on Chinese reading. English and sanitation are practically 5-period subjects; Bible and geography are 3-period-per-week subjects and history, a 2-period-per-week subject. Sewing and hand-work are reported as 1-period-per-week subjects.

The total number, 106 girls, in the Second Year Higher Primary grade reported their weekly recitations: 102 study mathematics (94 arithmetic, 7 mathematics, 1 algebra); 98 study Chinese reading; 94, history; 90, geography; 89, English; 88 Bible; and 63, physical training; 31, sewing; 20, sanitation; and 9, hand-work. The study of Mandarin is reported by 10 girls. Subjects for the most part given 5 periods per week are arithmetic, Chinese reading, and English; those given 3 periods per week are Bible, geography, and sanitation. Mandarin is usually given 2 periods per week. One girl reports sewing 2 periods per week; and 16, 1 period. History and hand-work are reported as 1-period-per-week subjects.

SUBJECTS OF STUDY—SECOND HIGHER PRIMARY

Number of Recitation Periods Per Week	1	2	3	4	5	6	7	8	9	10	12	13	14	Blanks	Total
Chinese Reading		2	15	3	34	2	12	1	2			1		26	98
Arithmetic		22			49					3				15	94
History	32	9	17	14	2									20	94
Geography	10	11	42		5									22	90
English		12	3	2	49					2	1		1	19	89
Bible		11	27	6	16									28	88
Physical Training	2	32	11	5	5									12	67
General Science	2	37	3	5	3									6	56
Writing	8	14	3	2	16	2								9	54
Music	19	15	2											1	37
Singing	18	3	4		2									7	34
Sewing	16	11												4	31
Drawing	12	13												4	29
Composition	10	4		1	10									1	26
Classics	2	5	1	1	3		1							12	25
Essays	14	5	2											4	25
Sanitation	1	1	3		2									13	20
Art	5	1	3		8									2	19
Ethics	3	3	8	2										3	19
Moral Training		12			3									4	19
Romanized	11														11
Mandarin		9		1											10
Hand-work	5		1	1										1	9
Manual Training		9													9
Letter Writing	7		1												8
Physiology				3	3									2	8
Mathematics					6		1								7
Grammar		1			2									3	6
Physics		3													3
Mencius					2										2
Piano				1										1	2
Rhetoric	1	1													2
Algebra					1										1
Five Books					1										1

Number in grade, 106; number reporting schedules, 106.

In the Third Year Higher Primary, all of the girls, 42 in number, report weekly schedules: 42 report the study of history; 41 report mathematics (29 arithmetic, 1 algebra, 11 mathematics); 41, Bible, and English; 38, Chinese reading; 28, physical training; 21, writing; 20, geography and singing. Eleven study Mandarin; 12, hygiene; 12, hand-work; and 3, sanitation. Five periods are usually given to arithmetic, Chinese reading, and English; 3 periods to hygiene and sanitation; 2 periods to geography and history. Thirteen recited Bible 3 periods per week, and 12, 5 periods per week.

SUBJECTS OF STUDY—THIRD HIGHER PRIMARY

Number of Recitation Periods Per Week	1	2	3	4	5	6	7	8	9	10	Not Reporting	Total
History		13	4	6	8						11	42
Bible			13	6	12						10	41
English			4		25					2	10	41
Chinese Reading		1	4	1	20	1					11	38
Arithmetic		1			18						10	29
Physical Training		20		2							6	28
Writing	10	4			2						5	21
Geography	1	13	2		2						2	20
Singing	13	2									5	20
Music	3	11									2	16
Classics		1		7	6	1						15
Composition	3		1	1	8	2						15
Hand-work	10	2										12
Hygiene			12									12
Essay	2		3								6	11
Mandarin					11							11
Mathematics					11							11
Romanized	10											10
Grammar											6	6
Sanitation			2		1							3
Biology					2							2
Algebra					1							1
Drawing		1										1
Ethics					1							1
General Science			1									1
Moral Training	1											1
Physical Geography											1	1
Letter Writing		1										1

Number of girls in grade, 42; number reporting schedules, 42.

The studies most frequently reported by the pupils in the primary schools are arithmetic, English, Chinese reading and writing, Bible, geography, and history. These subjects are studied, in every grade, although history is not studied by a large number until the first year higher primary. Five recitation periods each week are usually given to arithmetic, English, Chinese reading and writing; 2 or 3 periods to Bible, history, and geography. Physical training is reported by a large number in the lower primary grades, but drops to a secondary place in the last four years. The subjects of hygiene and sanitation, sewing, hand-work, and manual training are studied by relatively few pupils.

The schedules of the girls in the four years of the middle school follow in order.

SUBJECTS OF STUDY—FIRST MIDDLE SCHOOL

Number of Recitation Periods Per Week	1	2	3	4	5	6	7	8	9	10	11	12	Not Reporting	Total
Bible	12	18	8	2	8								13	61
Algebra		14	17		8	2							15	56
History	1	14	14	2	18								6	55
Singing	15	18	6	1	6								3	49
English	1		3	3	18		1			2			15	43
Physical Training	8	17	3	1	11	1							1	42
Chinese Literature	3	3		2	20			3					9	40
Composition	4	28	2	1	2									37
Grammar		8	15		9								2	34
Writing	5	3	8		4								4	24
Drawing	23													23
Essay	10												10	20
Arithmetic	8	3	6	1	1									19
Classics		6	2	7	3									18
Reading			4	1	5			1			1		6	18
Music	6	5	3		1	1								16
French		14												14
Biology		2	6		5									13
Education	3	5											4	12
Physiology	1	10												11
Chinese History		1	1		2								6	10
Chemistry		3	6		1									10
Sanitation	1				1								8	10
General Science			6	2										8
House Management	8													8
Physics		1	5											6
Piano	4				1								1	6
Sewing	1												5	6
Botany		6												6
Geography			2		3									5
Calculus		4												4
Cooking	3	1												4
Domestic Science		4												4
Astronomy		3												3
Household Arts	3													3
Mandarin	2	1												3
Geometry		2												2
General History					1								1	2
Letter-Writing	1												1	2
Moral Training					2									2
Biography					1									1
English Composition			1											1
Expression			1											1
Mencius					1									1

Number in grade, 74; number reporting schedules, 74.

SUBJECTS OF STUDY—SECOND MIDDLE SCHOOL

Number of Recitation Periods Per Week	1	2	3	4	5	6	7	8	9	10	Not Reporting	Total
English		1	13	11	40	5	1			3	18	92
Bible	7	17	15	17	9	1					17	83
History	1	24	20	9	9	2					10	75
Physical Training	16	28	12		10						7	73
Chinese Literature	2	8	10	21	5					2	9	57
Algebra		5	13	7	9	10					12	56
Composition	8	27	2	7							6	50
Singing	24	4	9	1	1						8	49
Geometry		12	11		5						8	36
Grammar		7	3	7	13	1					2	33
Physical Geography	1	3	6		16	1					4	31
Classics	1	4	9							3	13	30
Writing	16				5						9	30
Drawing	18	8	1									27
Reading	1				13			6	1			21
Physiology	1	6	12								1	20
Essay Writing	13	2									4	19
Education		11	6				1					18
Chemistry		2	9	6								17
Geology		8	1								6	15
Music	2	4	1	1	4						3	15
House Management	12	2										14
Mandarin	12	1										13
Arithmetic	1	2	6	1							1	11
History of Education	1	2	3	5								11
Botany		10										10
General History		1	1		5						3	10
Piano	1										9	10
General Science			10									10
Calculus		4	4		1							9
American Literature	1										7	8
Domestic Science		8										8
Astronomy		7										7
French		7										7
Psychology		7										7
Teaching of Drawing	1	6										7
Cooking	6											6
Chinese History			2								2	4
Sewing			1								2	3
Geography		1									1	2
Moral Training	2											2
Sanitation											2	2
Normal Training		1	1									2
Conversation			1									1
Embroidery		1										1
History of Literature			1									1
Oratory		1										1
Zoölogy		1										1

SUBJECTS OF STUDY—THIRD MIDDLE SCHOOL

Number of Recitation Periods Per Week	1	2	3	4	5	6	7	8	9	10	Not Reporting	Total
Bible	1	2	9	2	2					3	15	34
English	1	1	1	6	4					6	15	34
Chinese Literature	1	4	2	1	3						8	19
Essay	9	3		1							4	17
Singing	6				5						6	17
Geometry		1									5	15
History			6	2	2						4	14
Writing				1	4						9	14
Classics		1	7		1						5	14
Psychology	1	5	1								6	13
Chemistry			1								9	10
Composition	1	4									5	10
Physical Training	2	4			3							9
General Science			3		3						2	8
Physiology					7							7
Chinese Reading				1	5							6
Piano			3		1			1			1	6
House Management	4	1										5
Mandarin	5											5
Physics			5									5
Ancient Literature											5	5
Algebra			1			1					2	4
General History					1						3	4
Zoölogy											4	4
Arithmetic			2								1	3
English History			1	1	1							3
Music	2					1						3
Sanitation		2									1	3
Astronomy		2										2
Grammar		2										2
Hand-work	2											2
History of Bible			1		1							2
Moral Training	1				1							2
Physical Geography											2	2
Trigonometry			2									2
Drawing	2											2
Botany				1								1
Geography											1	1
Hygiene				1								1
Letter Writing	1											1
Sewing											1	1
English Stories					1							1
Debate	1											1

Number of girls in grade, 38; number reporting schedules, 37.

SUBJECTS OF STUDY—FOURTH MIDDLE SCHOOL

Recitation Periods Per Week	1	2	3	4	5	6	7	8	9	10	11	13	15	Not Reporting	Total
English		1		3	19	3	2	2		10		1	1	9	51
Chinese Literature		2	2	14	18	1								9	46
Bible	2		10	15	7									8	42
Chemistry		2	23		1									6	32
History	1	20	3	1	1									3	29
Mandarin	7	2	14	1											24
Composition	3	12	3	1	1										20
Essay Writing	14	3												2	19
Classics		3	5		5									5	18
Grammar		3			13									1	17
Methods of Teaching		5	2		9										16
Geometry		3	7		2										12
Music	7			1	1									1	10
Ethics		1	3		1									1	6
Arithmetic					2									3	5
Algebra		1	1			2					1				5
Hand-work					2									2	4
Normal Training					2									2	4
Moral Training		1			2										3
Astronomy		2													2
Geography	1	1													2
Drawing	2														2
Foreign History		2													2
Conversation		1													1

Number of girls in grade, 58; number reporting schedules, 54.

In the higher schools, algebra, geometry, and mathematics largely replace arithmetic; Chinese literature replaces Chinese reading. The sciences of biology, botany, chemistry, and physics replace geography; English and the Bible continue throughout. The tendency toward the newer subjects of sewing, household arts, household management, sanitation and hygiene may be traced in these schools as well as in the lower ones, and occasionally professional educational subjects are introduced in the last three years.

The schedules of the students in normal preparatory and normal schools are reported as follows:

SUBJECTS OF STUDY—NORMAL SCHOOL PREPARATORY

Recitation Periods Per Week	1	2	3	4	5	6	7	8	9	10	Not Reporting	Total
Arithmetic			1	1	4							6
Chinese Literature			1			4	1					6
Geography	5	1										6
Music	1	5										6
Physical Training			6									6
Drawing		6										6
Writing	1	1		4								6
Composition		5										5
History	4	1										5
Moral Training		5										5
Sewing			5									5
Chemistry		1										1
Education		1										1
Essay Writing		1										1
Hand-work		1										1
History of Literature		1										1
Zoölogy		1										1

Number of girls in grade, 6; number reporting schedules, 6.

SUBJECTS OF STUDY—FIRST NORMAL

Recitation Periods Per Week	1	2	3	4	5	6	7	8	9	10	11	12	13	14	Total
Composition	7	9													16
Arithmetic			1	4	3	5									13
Chinese Reading	2	5	2	4											13
Music	2	9	1	1											13
Bible	4	1	5	1											11
Geography		5	1	3	1										10
History of Education			10												10
Drawing	6	3													9
History		4		3											7
Classics		2	6												8
Physical Training	1	2	3		1										7
Psychology		7													7
Methods of Study	1	4	1												6
English	1	3				1									5
Methods of Teaching		1	4												5
General Science	1		1	1	1										4
Hand-work	1		3												4
Moral Training	2	2													4
Algebra					2	1									3
Botany		1		2											3
Chinese Literature					3										3
Physiology			3												3
Sewing		3													3
Writing		3													3
Kindergarten		1													1
English History		1													1
Education	1														1
Mother Play		1													1
Practice Teaching Bible					1										1
Practice Teaching Geography			1												1

Number of girls in grade, 17; number reporting schedules, 17.

SUBJECTS OF STUDY—SECOND NORMAL

Recitation Periods Per Week	1	2	3	4	5	6	7	8	9	10	14	15	16	18	20	Not Reporting	Total
Chinese Reading	1	2	4	8	1		2	5									23
Physical Training	7	2	10	2													21
Arithmetic			10		4	5											19
English		3	9		6							1					19
History		19															19
Education		8	10														18
Chemistry		8	2		7												17
Geography		10			5											2	17
Composition	7	5	3		1												16
Bible		10	5														15
Music	1	12	2														15
Practice Teaching		5			1	1				1	1	1	1	1	1		13
Drawing	2	9															11
Hand-work	1	9															10
Moral Training	2	8															10
Sewing		8			1												10
Chinese Literature		3	6														9
Writing	9																9
Singing		1	1				7										9
Mandarin		8															8
Grammar		7															7
Physics		6															6
Physiology		1	1		1											1	4
Psychology	1	2		1													4
General Science			2	1													3
Essay		2															2
Botany		1															1
Kindergarten		1															1
Mencius			1														1
Methods of Teaching			1														1
Zoölogy		1															1

Number of girls in grade, 29; number reporting schedules, 28.

SUBJECTS OF STUDY—THIRD NORMAL

Recitation Periods Per Week	1	2	3	4	5	6	7	8	9	10	Not Reporting	Total
Chemistry		1	4	6								11
Physical Training	2	4	5									11
Sewing		11										11
Education	5		5									10
History		6	3		1							10
English			2			5				1		8
Music	1	7										8
Chinese Reading		4		3								7
Bible		6										6
Composition			1	5								6
Household Management		6										6
Magazine	6											6
Arithmetic		2	3									5
Geography		5										5
Letter Writing	5											5
Hand-work	2	2										4
Poetry	4											4
Writing	3	1										4
Chinese Literature			3									3
Essay Writing		3										3
Grammar	2	1										3
Singing		3										3
Zoölogy		3										3
Classics	2											2
Drawing			2									2
Home-work	2											2
Mandarin		2										2
Moral Training		2										2
Physics		2										2

Number of girls in grade, 11; number reporting schedules, 11.

In the normal schools the. subjects of the lower schools are reviewed. To these education, history of education, kindergarten, methods of study, methods of teaching, practice teaching, practice teaching of geography and Bible and psychology are added. The data from the Normal Schools are inadequate for a definite study.

IMPORTANT SUBJECTS OF THE CURRICULUM—REPORTED BY 1119 SCHOOLGIRLS

Number of Recitation Periods Per Week	1	2	3	4	5	6	7	8	9	10	11	12	13	14	15	Periods Not Reported	Totals
Liberal Arts Subjects:																	
Chinese Classics and Literature	29	124	154	100	296	34	44	16	15	23		1	2			297	1135
English	14	81	78	51	419	50	7	8		37		3	3	1	2	232	986
Mathematics	20	164	183	53	359	36	12			4	1		1			190	1043
Bible	34	142	219	84	161	8				5		1				236	890
History	52	266	128	84	71	5				1						148	761
Geography	39	184	141	34	108	1										164	671
Science	17	192	93	56	28	3										63	452
Chinese Composition	71	84	9	14	31	2										10	211
Practical Arts Subjects:																	
Sewing	53	63	13	1	1											25	156
Hand-work	84	35	7	3	7											12	148
Sanitation	19	8	17		11											34	89
Domestic Science	51	28															79
Hygiene		13	12	7												5	39
Manual Training	5	9														1	15
Cooking	4																4
Professional Educational Subjects:																	
Psychology	2	22	1	1												7	33
Education	6	9	16														31
(14 15 16 18 20)										(14)	(15)	(16)	(18)	(20)			
Practice Teaching		6	1	5	5	1		1		2	1	1	1	1			22
History of Education	1	2	3	5													11
Methods of Teaching		1	5													1	7
Methods of Study	1	5	1														7
Kindergarten Training		3			1												4

When the courses of study are considered as a unit, it becomes apparent that out of the 1119 girls reporting, there are 1135,[1] reports on Chinese reading, classics and literature; 986, or 88.1 per cent, report English and grammar; 890, or 86.7 per cent, Bible; 1042, or 93.2 per cent, mathematics; 761, or 68 per cent, history; 671, or 59.9 per cent, geography; 452, or 40.3 per cent, science; 302, or 26.9 per cent, domestic science in its various phases; 128, or 11.4 per cent, hygiene and sanitation; and 115, or 10.2 per cent, subjects in normal training.

[1] Two hundred and twenty-six report Chinese classics, 521 report Chinese reading, and 388 report Chinese literature.

Mathematics, Chinese, English, Bible, history, and science are thus the predominating subjects. Unquestionably each one of these supplies in some degree a demand of society. Arithmetic, Chinese—the mother tongue of the pupils—religion, science, and history, are all integral parts of the life experience of every Chinese girl. English is an important medium in all higher education to-day. Moreover, among the business and professional classes it is desired for intercourse with powerful foreigners who live in every important city.

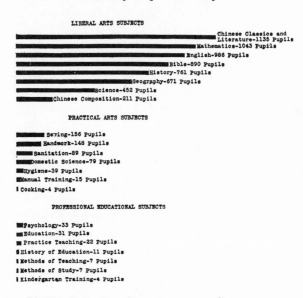

FIG. 7. IMPORTANT SUBJECTS OF THE CURRICULUM.

In an analysis of the curriculum, however, it is evident that the schedule, especially in the lower grades, is very heavily loaded. The study of the Chinese language—character reading, writing and composition—is extremely difficult in spite of the fact that it is the mother tongue of the pupils. Ability to read the literature which is considered essential for scholars, or even ability to read the newspapers and magazines, is rarely acquired without years of intensive work. To this subject are added, even in the lower primary school, history, science, mathematics and foreign language. In the mission schools Bible completes the schedule. The mitigating features of the situation are that the girls in school at the present time are from four to six years older than the normal ages in the lower grades, and that they are probably a highly selected group intellectually as well as socially. It is to be expected, however, that the work will be too severe for the younger group of perhaps average intelligence which will come into the schools in increasing numbers. To relieve this overloading, the requirements in Chinese may be modified,[1] parts of arithmetic and higher mathematics omitted, since the theory of formal discipline can no longer justify their continuance as a subject for study in the lower grades, large portions of Western history supplanted by history of the nations of the Far East, and science applied to daily experience. To evaluate every portion of every subject in the curriculum; to discard the useless and to keep only that part which is applicable to the lives of the Chinese schoolgirls; to experiment, to test the results of every change, and to adopt only the best,—is an imperative need of education for girls in China to-day.

The reduction of the present course of study is made more necessary to provide time for the important subjects, now neglected, which should be emphasized in the curriculum. Since only 36.4 per cent of the girls are studying subjects which relate directly either to the home or to community life,[2] since the majority of the girls live away from home most of the years they attend school thus having little opportunity to obtain training in household science, and since each of the girls will become a part of some social group after completing the school course, there is evident need for a closer relation of the curriculum to immediate home and community life. With the present system, maladjustments in family and village are frequent. Mothers-in-law often dread the new order of courtship by which a son brings into the home a Western trained daughter-in-law who cannot cook and despises housework. Many schoolgirls dread marriage as a "prison-house," and welcome any plan which will free them from the responsibility and meaningless drudgery of housekeeping. In one village the daughter so evidently disapproved her mother's

---

[1] Chinese educators have already given much attention to this subject, and have introduced readers containing selections from literature and the classics. Many are also working upon the problem of the character.

[2] Only 26.3 per cent are studying domestic science, 10.8 per cent, hygiene and sanitation, and none, sociology or civics.

way of doing things that the mother broke up the home, sent all of the children to boarding school, and went herself to a women's training school. The benefits derived from a school curriculum which separates pupils from life and gives neither appreciation of nor training in the fundamental processes of home keeping may be definite and measurable, but they are accompanied by great and unnecessary evils.

Furthermore, such a curriculum is directly opposed to the trend of modern educational theory and practice. The worth of any curriculum to-day is judged, not by precision and uniformity of subject matter, but by its contribution to the life and growth of each child as an individual in society. This demands that "nature and society live in the schoolroom" and that the "forms and tools of learning" be "subordinated to the substance of experience."[1] This may be obtained by making the home and the community vital factors in the experience of the pupil during the years spent at school. The introduction of courses in household subjects with projects which bring the girls into close contact with their homes, and courses in sociology, based on experimental studies of Chinese villages, is both possible and necessary in the socialization of the curriculum.

Courses are also needed to prepare women to render definite service under the changing condition of Chinese society. The Chinese schoolgirls have signified their purposes to become physicians, nurses, and teachers. The rise of the normal schools, and the introduction of professional subjects in the secondary schools, show that the demand for preparation for teaching as a vocation is becoming already insistent. It will not be long before the need for training in other vocations will be equally imperative. It is true that complete preparation for vocations and professions cannot be accomplished in secondary schools. On the other hand, however, courses that will help in the first few years of teaching, community aids in sanitation, hygiene, nursing, and domestic economy are possible in every higher primary and middle school program. An essential part of the secondary school curriculum is to give each girl a broad foundation of knowledge and thought. But it is equally important that it en-

---

[1] Dewey, *School and Society*, p. 56.

able her to prepare for some phase of effective social helpfulness whenever she is compelled to leave school.

The fundamental reorganization of the curricula to provide more reasonable programs, closer relation to community and home life, and more definite preparation for service, in order that the girls in the schools may receive an adequate opportunity for study, is an immediate task for educators in China.

CHAPTER V

CONCLUSION

Summary of Results

The education of girls in China has been a definite, comparatively conscious process for many centuries. Among the upper classes the more fortunate women have been accomplished, and have learned to read and to write. Some have become artists and great scholars. But the majority of women, from ancient times down to the present day, have known little of the world outside of the inner courts of their own homes.

For over nine hundred and ninety out of every thousand girls in China to-day, education means obedience to older members of the family and self-training to compliance in all requests. For many of these it means also learning to spin linen from flax and silk from cocoons, to weave cotton, to make garments for every member of the family: garments of single thickness for summer, and of double thickness padded with cotton for winter; to supply hats for the men and shoes for all, to cook food with a stubble fire, to manage a family of six on an income below a living wage. There is little time, little thought, and no opportunity for learning to read.

The first school for girls which introduced Western subjects was started by a missionary in 1843. Very gradually the idea of schools for girls permeated the nation. In 1876, the increase of numbers attending began to become apparent. In 1898 the first school under Chinese management was opened as a private institution. In 1907 the government established a system of schools for the education of girls. But since the first revolution in 1911, there has been a phenomenal rise in the number of girls attending mission, private and government schools, and institutions are unable to accommodate those who apply for admission. In spite of this fact, however, probably fewer than ten in one thousand girls are attending school. It is estimated that eight out of the ten are in the first four years of the course. Approximately seven girls out of ten thousand are attending the higher

84

primary school, and three in ten thousand are pursuing a course in the middle school.   These girls are in day and boarding institutions situated for the most part in great cities along trade routes.

From the study of one thousand one hundred and seventy-six of the pupils of the boarding schools it may be concluded that the schoolgirls of China to-day are a very highly selected class.   Their fathers are usually professional and business men whose incomes are between $500 and $600 Mexican per year.   Over one half of the girls live in dormitories, and thus are separated from their homes, except for brief visits, during their entire course in higher primary, middle and normal schools.   In the investigation of the ambitions of this group it was found that almost one third desire to teach.

The majority of the girls are from ten to eighteen years of age.   They enter school from four to six years older than the legal entrance age.   In the first year of the lower primary school, and in every year thereafter, a large proportion are over-age. While in school, the girls study Chinese literature, composition and writing; mathematics, and English, history, geography, and science and in mission schools, Bible.   Usually five recitation periods each week are given to the five subjects, four periods to history, and three periods to the last three subjects.   A few girls report one or two recitations each week in sewing, household arts, hygiene and sanitation.   In the middle school some give time to professional educational subjects.

RECOMMENDATIONS

In view of the vast number of girls still unreached by the schools, a definite program for securing universal school attendance needs to be worked out by the authorities in government, private and mission educational systems.   If feasible, these three agencies should follow one central plan adopted by all, after a careful, extensive survey of the situation in each province. Such a provincial survey and plan would include a census of the population of children of school age and available schools with the present school attendance, and would definitely endeavor to reach large, now untouched geographical areas.

Where union provincial plans are impossible, surveys of local cities and villages, showing the distribution of population, occupation of citizens, wealth, present school attendance, and classes from which students come, carried on by voluntary associations of resident educators, may be accomplished in many educational centers. Some of the results which might be expected from such a survey are: a definite plan for providing educational facilities for now neglected districts, a basis for estimating a feasible scheme for financing the schools, and systematic. propaganda among all social classes which will enlist their enthusiastic support and secure a consciousness of the possibility of and desire for the education of every child. That there is increasing interest in the problem of education is evident from the sudden rise of the number of pupils in school. This interest should be utilized in furthering the rapid extension of schools in the democracy of the East.

It is evident from the investigation of this study that special attention must be given to attendance problems in farmer, artisan and laborer classes. It is necessary that some arrangement be made for the support of girls in school in order that the daughters of these great untouched, poverty-burdened classes be given opportunity for education. Free schools are not yet provided, for there is no national system of taxation for education,[1] and the sources of revenue are entirely inadequate to finance the needed rapid increase in the number of schools. At the same time, the extreme poverty of great masses of people will doubtless prevent them from supporting either the schools or the children while at school. This problem of finance is one of the greatest which faces educators in China to-day, and will continue until the economic status of the people be raised by the wide use of natural resources, and until the public demand and furnish education for all children.

There is also definite need that educational institutions find some way by which the pupils during their years of education may be brought into close contact with both home and society. Wherever possible, the pupils attending school should live at home or with relatives. Home projects in household work, in sanitation, in entertainment through synopses of history, geography or literature lessons, and home reading of the newspapers, should be definitely planned and executed. Parents and friends may be

---

[1] Kuo, P. W., *Chinese Education System*, pp. 133, 147.

invited often to the schools and made the guests of groups, classes or the whole school. For girls who must live at the school, a "model house" in which home problems may be carried on should be an essential of institutional equipment. For older pupils, and those in the higher primary or middle grades, projects which will involve study in neighboring villages will give perspective to students. By these, and many other methods and by constantly growing experimentation the girls may be kept vital factors in society while at school.

Moreover, there is need for courses which give definite preparation for some vocation. The changing social order already demands new types of education for the Chinese girl. Schools are opened in rapidly increasing numbers. For every school a teacher is needed, and these teachers must be trained. To the end that they may not drop into a dull routine, bounded by tradition and limited by the class-room walls, the girls who have expressed a desire to enter this profession should study the principles of education, and have opportunity for supervised practice before leaving school. This will at least awaken in them a professional consciousness, and make growth in service a probability. In many communities there is also need for the social service or evangelistic worker. Schools may introduce courses in religion and civic betterment that will definitely fit girls for this work in villages and cities. Business is beginning to make a place for women, and business courses may supply the need of some girls. Probably special schools for advanced study in social service, commerce, and industry will be developed later, as they have been for education. Until vocational schools are within the reach of every girl, courses which will train girls for the work they must do are a necessity, that girls who leave school before they reach the higher professional schools will be fitted to render some immediate contribution to their communities.

In order that time may not be wasted, a universal entrance age at six or seven years should be secured through propaganda and law enforcement. A close articulation of the systems of government, private and mission schools to provide efficient transfer and the adjustment of each year schedule of study to the actual ability of the pupils. This will involve an attendance department (perhaps working under a union committee), which will seek to stimulate public opinion on school attendance, which will investigate absences and visit the homes of non-attending children of school age. It will involve a comparison and evolution of the various courses of study throughout each city, and official recognition of every school. It will necessitate the careful study of the progress[1] of every pupil and class, and the constant change of curriculum requirements. There will be need for extremely flexible grade divisions, frequent promotions, wide individual choice of subject matter with special rooms for those who are either especially gifted or backward.

Instead of the overloaded and artificial curriculum of Chinese reading and writing—the mastery of which is in itself a gigantic task—plus the Western subjects of arithmetic, foreign language, Bible, history, geography and science, a curriculum of studies fitted to the needs of the Chinese girl is imperative. Let the traditional divisions of the curriculum be questioned, and let only those things be taught which the pupil, the community, or the nation demand for physical and spiritual well-being and growth. If the schoolgirl must read books, magazines and newspapers, teach her the characters used in their vocabularies. If for efficiency in the school or home, in cooking or household management, she should understand and apply the laws of heat, light or food changes, direct her to her environment for the problems which she will meet daily in the process of living. She would keep herself in good health: discuss with her its laws, and make the practice of these laws an essential to successful completion of the course. If she has an opportunity to assist in cleaning up a house or a village, help her to understand and execute the principles of sanitation. If she desires to speak with foreign people, or to read a foreign literature, teach her those words and phrases which she will need. When she becomes conscious of interests of her village as a part of the world interests, and would study places and customs and trade, lead her into the problems of geography. When knowledge of the development of her own and other nations will add to the richness of her experience and the comprehension of present-day movements, direct her into the study of history.

---

[1] The real progress of pupils in subjects has been measured in America, and some places of China, by the standard tests. Only a very few—perhaps those in arithmetic, drawing and sewing, are fitted for translation, but tests in various subjects if such could be made would be very valuable in providing objective measures of achievement.

When she seeks the meanings of world tendencies, of individual life and the relation of belief and action discuss with her the interpretations and questions of religion and philosophy Give time for appreciation of sunset and river, melody and beauty. In all of these essentials of living it is the privilege of the school to help. But the worth of the school curriculum is not determined by its precision or completeness of outline, but by its actual contribution to the growth of the child who studies. Such a course of study prepares for continual as well as for ultimate service. It calls for a fundamental reorganization of the present curriculum based upon experimental investigation of the present needs of the community, and the life needs of the Chinese schoolgirl.

The womanhood of China to-day faces a new world. Soon, perhaps in this generation, the age-old duty of clothing her family will be entirely taken away from her, the burdens of the housekeeping lightened by modern inventions and the standards of living raised because of increased incomes. Citizenship, perhaps enfranchised citizenship, in a republic will bring responsibilities to women as individuals and will push the boundaries of their thought life far beyond the walls of their villages. Bridges, electric power plants, mines and railroads will shatter belief in superstitions and make way for faith. Ethical relationships, and righteous conduct, emphasized for millenniums but limited to the family, may be broadened to those altruistic attitudes which link ambition for self improvement with an unselfish purpose for service.

To those who have undertaken the task of guiding education for women in this generation belongs the task of experiment, measurement and adjustment which will give the new woman, through contact with life situations, a vision of her possibilities. Thus may the woman of new China be prepared in knowledge, skill, and spirit to serve her home, her community, her nation and the world.

BIBLIOGRAPHY

ENGLISH

Bashford, J. W. *China, an Interpretation.*

Beach, H. P. and St. John, B. *World Atlas of Christian Missions.* (1910.)

Bland, J. O. P. and Backhouse, E. W. *China Under the Empress Dowager.*

Boggs, L. Pearl. *Chinese Womanhood.*

Burton, Margaret S. *The Education of Women in China.*

Burton, Margaret S. *Notable Women of Modern China.*

China Mission Handbook, The, 1896.

China Mission Year Books, The, 1910–1917.

China Year Books, The, 1912–1916.

Cubberley, E. P. *Public School Administration.*

Dean, W. *The China Mission.*

Dewey, John. *School and Society.*

Encyclopedia of Education.

Faber, E. *Famous Women of China.*

Gamewell, Mary Ninde. *The Gateway to China.*

Giles, H. A. *A History of Chinese Literature.*

Giles, L. *Alphabetical Index to the Chinese Encyclopedia.*

Goodsell, Willystine. *The Family.*

Headland, I. T. *Court Life in China.*

Headland, I. T. *Home Life in China.*

Kiang, S. C. *Women and Education in China.* (Unpublished.)

King, F. H. *Farmers of Forty Centuries.*

King, H. E. *Educational System of China as Recently Reconstructed.*

Kuo, P. W. *The Chinese System of Public Education.*

Kuo, P. W. *The Training of Teachers in China.* (Thesis, Teachers College, 1912.)

Little, Mrs. A. *In the Land of the Blue Gown.*

Pott, F. L. H. *A Sketch of Chinese History.*

Records of the General Conference of the Protestant Missionaries of China, 1877.

Reinsch, P. S. *Intellectual and Political Currents in the Far East.*

Reinsch, P. S. *New Education in China.* (Reprint from *Atlantic Monthly,* April, 1909.)

Reports of:

    American Baptist Missionary Union, 1856–1909.

    American Baptist Foreign Missionary Society, 1909–1917.

    American Board of Commissioners for Foreign Missions, 1833–1915.

    Board of Foreign Missions of the Methodist Episcopal Church, 1823–1915.

    Board of Foreign Missions of the Presbyterian Church, 1833–1917.

    Domestic and Foreign Missionary Society of the Protestant Episcopal Church of the United States of America, 1831–1917.

North China Woman's Conference of the Methodist Episcopal Church, 1917.

School Committee of Brighton, Mass., 1849–50.

Wesleyan Society.

Woman's American Baptist Foreign Missionary Society, 1874–1917.

Woman's Foreign Missionary Society of the Methodist Episcopal Church, 1873–1917.

Worlds Missionary Conference, 1910, Vol. III.   Christian Education.

Ross, E. A.   *The Changing Chinese.*

Saxelby, E. Mary.   *Woman's Work in Tientsin.*   (Pamphlet.)

Smith, A. H.   *Village Life in China.*

Strayer, G. D.   *Some Problems in City School Administration.*

Streit, P. C.   *Atlas Hierarchicus.*

Triennial Reports of the China Educational Association.   (1899–1902.)

Williams, S. W.   *History of China.*

Williams, S. W.   *Middle Kingdom.*

TRANSLATIONS

Confucious.   *Lun Yü* (Analects).   Translated by J. Legge.

I King (Book of Changes).   Translated by J. Legge.

Jen Hsiao.   *Nei Hsun* (Teaching of the Inner Courts).   Translated by I. T. Headland.   (Unpublished.)

Li Ki (Book of Rites).   Translated by J. Legge.

Lu Chow.   *Nü Heo* (Teaching for Women).   Translated in *The Chinese Repository*, Vol. IX.

Meng Tze (Mencius).   Translated by J. Legge.

San Tze King (Three Character Classic).   Translated in *The Chinese Repository*, Vol. IV.

She King (Book of Odes).   Translated by J. Legge.

Sung Jo Chao.   Nü Lun Yü (Analects for Women).   Translated by I. T. Headland.   (Unpublished.)

Tsao, Lady.   *Nü Chieh* (Instruction for Women).   Translated by I. T. Headland.   (Unpublished.)

Wang Chieh Fu.   *Nü Fan Chieh Lu* (Short Records of Exemplary Women).   Translated by I. T. Headland.   (Unpublished.)

CHINESE

Chiao Yu Pu Wen Tu Liao Piang (Educational Documents).

Chiao Yu Pu Wen Tu Lei Pien (Educational Documents).

Chiao Yu Pu Ching Chun Kao Teng Hsiao Hsueh Hsiao Ling (Orders Issued by the Board of Education on the Regulations for Higher Primary Schools).

Chiao Yu Pu Ching Chun Haiu Cheng Shih Fan Hsueh Hsiao Kwei Chu (Orders Issued by the Board of Education on the Regulations for Normal Schools).

Chung Hsueh Hsiao Ling (Regulations for Middle Schools).

Chung Hwa Min Kwoa Ti $\left\{ \begin{array}{c} I \\ Er \end{array} \right\}$ *Tze Chiao Yu Tung Chi Tu Piao* (Annual
    Statistical Reports of the Board of Education).   1912–13.
Ku Chin Tu Shu Chi Cheng (The Encyclopedia).
Kwoa Min Hsueh Hsiao Ling (Regulations for Citizens Schools).
Lu Hsiang.   *Lieh Nü Chwan* (Biographies of Eminent Women).

PERIODICALS

ENGLISH

Catholic Missions.
The Chinese Recorder.
The Chinese Repository.
The Chinese Students' Monthly.
The Educational Review.
The Spirit of Missions.
Women's Missionary Friend (formerly *Heathen Women's Friend*).
Woman's Work in the Far East.
Woman's Work for Women.

GERMAN

Zeitschaft für Missions-Wissenschaft.

CHINESE

The Chinese Weekly.
The Chinese Educational Review.